THE UNREVEALING SHADOW WALKER

Uncover Your Eyes to See
the Reality of the Mask of Lies

CATHERINE MARTIN

Copyright © 2025 Catherine Martin
All rights reserved
New Edition

Published By: Catherine Martin

ISBN 978-1-964452-46-3 (HardCover)
ISBN 978-1-964452-45-6 (SoftCover)
ISBN 978-1-964452-47-0 (Digital)

LCCN: 9781964452456

Printed in the United States of America

In loving memories of my mother
Overseer Mary L. Hardy
03/22/1948–02/10/2021

Your present, we miss, your memory, we treasure,

Loving you always
Forgetting you never

Mother and daughter

James C. Hardy Sr.

Family Love

Mary L. Hardy

James C. Hardy Jr.

Mrs. Catherine L. Hardy Martin

Mrs. Teresa E. Hardy Williams

See!
I will not forget you...
I have carved you on the palm of my hand.
Isaiah 49:15

DEDICATION

For all those who help me through my struggles and obstacles in my life. This book is dedicated to God, my belated mother Overseer Mary Hardy, my sons, Jaquan Scott, Steven Jr. and wife Tamara Sweeney, and stepdaughter Daziyah Rosebure, belated best friend Darnette Dickey and Lakiesha Davis, my sister Teresa Williams, belated father James C. Hardy Sr., and James C. Hardy Jr. and to everyone else who are going through and need advice, answers, or solutions. God is the key to all circumstances. He is the healer and problem fixer. He can resolve all problems if you just give him a chance and wait patiently on him. Listen, you do not know what the outcomes are going to be or look like when you do something out of the will of God, so stay in the race and trust the almighty King. Victory is waiting for those who trust, holding on and committing themselves to God. Please consult God first in everything that you do, get God's approval first because he knows what is best for our life.

I pray and believe that this book can be helpful to your soul. I hope that when you read this powerful, true life story that I have shared with you, it will cause deliverance, healing, restoration,

understanding, hope, and love to flow around your well-being. God is truly concern about your life. God loves you with his whole heart, and he is concerned about your soul. God loves you, and so do I. I am glad to be in the obeying to God to share my story or testimonies with the world.

These songs came into my head "I Don't Mind Waiting" by Juanita Bynum and "Better Days" by Le'Andria Johnson. Stay encouraged, and God bless. Amen.

Inspiration

What inspired me to write this book were the trials and tribulations I have endured in my life. It all began in 2008, during my college years, when God guided me to start writing. Writing allowed me to express the feelings in my heart, providing a release with every word I penned. I was navigating a terrible storm in my life, feeling stressed, worried, downhearted, and lonely. There was a point where I was ready to give up on everything, including myself, my family, my marriage, and my ministry; it felt like all odds were against me. However, I know that God sustained me when all hope seemed lost, and my spirit was slowly dying. Jeremiah 29:11 states, "For I know the plans I have for you, declares the Lord, plans to prosper you and not to harm you, plans to give you hope and a future." God taught me to trust His help, humble my spirit, and be patient.

God is a man of His word; He rescued my heart, mind, and soul, especially when I almost let the devil deceive me. I completely surrendered to God's will, not my own. It doesn't matter whether you are a Christian; as humans, we all face many obstacles in life. My way never worked out, but God's way showed me a different picture—one that was better and more peaceful. I allowed my blindfold to come off, beginning to hear and see the reality that God had a greater, loving plan for me. I learned that God is the only key to genuine love, salvation, strength, faith, healing, favor, and blessings. God's support comes with a guaranteed package. I obeyed God's call to share my story with the world as a Christian who has also faced difficult times, but for whom giving up was never an option. This wasn't a one-night ordeal; it was a process of healing. I cried and called out to God many times, and He has never failed me yet, as Psalm 120:1 says, "In my distress I cried to the Lord, and He heard me."

Relationships have become a significant issue in today's world. This is why I felt compelled to share my real-life encounters. Unaddressed, these issues can profoundly affect one's mental and physical well-being. I needed the world to understand that being in any kind of harmful relationship or situation is utterly unacceptable, especially from God's perspective. Remember, you are not alone; you are important, even when others make you feel unworthy. Acknowledging, recognizing, or admitting these issues marks the beginning of healing. Staying ashamed or blaming yourself won't set you free; it will only keep you bound for life. I am the beginning of my voice, and your voice, so let us all voice out together. "Let the roar inside come out, you can sound the alarm." Stand up and roar, people. You have the power within you to move forward as you please, with no turning back. I urge you to "reverse" your situation with God's help. I encourage you to put God first in your life. He may not come when you want Him, but He arrives right on time. I wanted my voice to matter, as God led me to do, to help other souls. Stay encouraged and keep the faith. Amen!

"Better Days" by Le'Andria Johnson

Sometimes it feels cold
And you feel all alone
But hold on, better days are coming
It can be rough in this world
I know it ain't easy but hang on in there
I know better days are coming
You seen good, you seen bad
You been hurt beyond sin
But just remember that better days
Better days are coming
Friends will leave you all by yourself
But don't cry
'Cause better days are coming, oh
Better days (better days)
Better days
Better days are coming
It's only a season
Hang on in for you going through, yeah
But stay focused and never lose sight
I know people, people
They don't see the hurt you feel inside
But keep on smiling 'cause everything will be alright
Better days (it's here now)
Better days (I feel it)
Better days are coming (you've got to believe in better days)
Better days (for your mother and your father and your sister and your brother)
Better days
Better days are coming
Hey yeah
Better days are coming
Better days are coming your way soon

"VERSES THAT IMPACTED MY LIFE"

Proverbs 16:1 and 7 remind us, "We can make our own plans, but the Lord gives the right answer... We can make our own plans, but the Lord determines our steps." So, don't settle for the mess in your life. Clean it up, and trust God for the best.

Deuteronomy 31:6 assures us, "He will never leave you nor forsake you." I strive for my love to reflect the love of my King, the Lord, who endured all things. No matter how I've been mistreated, I remember that my Father, too, was betrayed, lied about, cursed, persecuted, and crucified. Yet, Jesus stayed in the will of God and loved even His enemies, offering His life so that we might live.

When we love as Jesus did, even in the face of hurt and disappointment, we rise above the enemy's schemes. Love has the power to change hearts and break through the darkness. We are greater than any deceit or harm that comes our way. With the love of Christ, we can overcome anything.

If you don't know love, then you don't truly know God. As 1 Corinthians 13:4-8, 13 says: "Love is patient, love is kind. It does not envy, it does not boast, it is not proud. It does not dishonor others, it is not self-seeking, it is not easily angered, it keeps no record of wrongs... Love never fails." Let the mind of Christ guide your heart always.

By focusing on God and His work, I've found the strength to stay alive and well. His love never fails.

Chapter 1

THE UNREVEALING SHADOW WALKER UNCOVER YOUR EYES TO SEE THE REALITY OF THE MASK OF LIES

Uncover your eyes and see the true reality that sits like watchmen on the wall, lurking out your desires, needs, and wants. God is the true light to the waking of your soul. He does not blindside you away from reality. Watch out, the 3D illusion can bring you into a make-believe world of delusions. Now you are fighting against what is real or not into your own wants, needs, and desires. The unrevealing shadow walker can screenplay you right into your own fantasy world by having your eyes close to a fake unknown world. Your mind has been driven into a deep coma, and now you only feel and see your dreams of what you want to imagine into an unrealistic world. Ouch! (I have been pinched.) My wake-up call came right on time.

Chapter 2

THE MASK OF THE UNREVEALING SHADOW WALKER OF A HUMAN BEING FORM
I COME IN MANY DISGUISES AND FORMS BEFORE YOUR EYES

I can camouflage as church attire, thug look, nerdy, shy, educator, wealthy, unfortunate one, incarcerated, poor struggling, pity, and famous I will come through your own attraction that catches you off guard. You will never see me because you are too in touch with your own desires, needs, and wants that catch you off your feet.

The mask of the unrevealing shadow walker

I can be whatever part your desires seek because I know your weakness. I did not come from heaven to save, rebuild, make whole, deliver, love, or join in matrimony (marriage). I came from hell to destroy, separate, keep bound, cause division, show hatred, kill, control, and capture your soul. The enemy looks at your soul as food for doomed to hell. It hungers after souls to satisfy the lake of fire (eternal flame). It serves no good when coming after your life. So stop thinking evil is your friend or buddy because it shows your eyes. It is doing justice to meet the desires of your needs. You have been punked or played.

However, you will not or cannot let me go because I make you feel good (unrevealing shadow walker). You were told by your spouse, boyfriend, friends, or family that you cannot get anybody else because they do not want you. It says that you're unattractive, you're too fat, too skinny, too tall, too short, your hair too short or too long, you're not worth it, you're not good enough, you're going to grow old by yourself, or you're lucky someone loves you and want you. I have you recording in your mind and saying it out of your mouth, "He loves me," "He takes care of me," I don't like being alone," "He got a job, and he pays the bills." No, the unrevealing shadow walker wants you to believe and receive that he cares and loves you that way, but in all actuality, it's all in the master plans of the mask of the unrevealing shadow walker of a human being form.

Your needs have drawn him by your luxurious heatwave to the attraction of your lack of areas of desires that you seek. You have been taken off your course of focus, which you are now at a vulnerable stage. You're open to believe, hear, and see what the unrevealing shadow walker has presented in your mind. He is the mask of lies of the deceitful shadow walker. He covers the eyes of he who blinded your view from reality.

The mask of lies.

Do not let the shadow walker catch you off balance. It will steal your life.

Uncover your eyes. Love does not cause pain or drama in a relationship or life itself. This is the hands of the enemy work. That is not the blessing of God.

Chapter 3

THE SHADOW WALKER

There is not one of us who has not been
taken in by a shadow walker. What is this thing that causes so
much distress in our lives?
A shadow walker is a person who wears many masks.
(We shall use the empirical "he" here not to
denote gender, but for simplicity.)
He is the person who oozes charm to everyone he meets.
He offers help and assistance, support, loving kindness.
He is the perfect goodwill ambassador with lofty ideals,
great concern for the welfare of mankind,
and a deep belief in the brotherhood of all people.
What a wonderful person! You get to know him.
You relax around him, begin to rely upon
his word and his judgment.
You confide in him about your work,
your family life, and the most personal aspects of yourself.
He is your friend. He would do anything for you.
You trust him. He is not real.
It is a mask he wears in public
that has nothing to do with the reality of who he is.

Catherine Martin

The shadow walker will take all your
confidences and use them against you.
He begins to gossip about you.
He twists your words to use to his own best advantage.
He makes false accusations about you, and
because everyone knows what a wonderful and caring person
he is, he is believed.
He steals your thoughts, words,
and the plans you may have shared with
him and makes them his own.
He takes full credit while laughing at you for being a fool.
You have been betrayed.
He takes advantage of every good thing he has learned about
you
and then turns his back on you. He is finished with you.
You have nothing more for him to take.
He moves on to his next mark,
oozing charm and self-confidence.
The shadow walker is dangerous.
He has destroyed marriages, relationships,
stolen lives,
cost some their jobs,
and driven some to violence, alcoholism, drug abuse, or
suicide.
More often than not,
the shadow walker is the product of an environment,
which battered his own view of himself until
he was convinced that he had no value.
His self-esteem and feelings of personal value
and self-worth have been virtually destroyed.
At some point, he has learned to lie, to steal, to manipulate
and to "con" in order to create an image of
the person he considers successful. He does this by absorb-
ing the heart,
Spirit, and essence of those he admires but can never be.
Nothing is beyond him, and nothing is sacred to him.
He has learned how to create the mask that
will give him access to people he considers valuable to him.

He actively searches them out.

The Unrevealing Shadow Walker

He uses them up and throws them away.
How do you fight a shadow walker?
You cannot.
Once you have been chosen as his mark,
everything you do will be used against you.
If you speak out against him,
you will only arouse sympathy in others for him.
If you try to fight him, they will defend him.
He is a master at his game,
and you do not even know the rules.
The natural reaction is to strike back in anger
and righteous indignation.
The need for revenge is strong.
You have been betrayed at every level of your being,
and the hurt you feel is intense.
Sometimes,
a financial loss may also be involved.
If there is legal action you can take, then take it
and leave the details of the battle to others.
I have worked or being a witness with many people
who have suffered at the hands of such deceivers.
The only way to effectively deal with a shadow walker
is to distance yourself,
cut your losses, learn your lesson, and walk away.
Rebuild your own dignity and value as a human being.
Do not allow your feelings against the shadow
walker to alter your dealings
with other honorable and ethical people.
Control the impulse to be overly suspicious
and distrustful of everyone.
It is a natural survival instinct after such an experience,

but remember what life was like before the shadow walker.
You are a good and honorable person.
This is the belief and attitude
that will carry you through the ordeal.
Be strong, for you walk in the light.

Catherine Martin

—Author Unknown

This is an official sovereign Amonsoquath Band of Cherokee government sponsored web site page maintained by Rainbow Eagle Woman.

Chapter 4

CHOOSE UNTIL THIS DAY: "YOU HAVE A CHOICE TO TAKE FLIGHT 111 TO HEAVEN OR FRIGHT 666 TO HELL"

THE CHOICE IS IN YOUR HANDS HEAVEN OR HELL

The shadow walker is a connection to the nonexistent world to hell. The shadow walker walks in the world (human-being form) as an unclean spirit to whom he can befoul whoever it seeks. It is ready to use its charm of hospitality to work its way into your human soul. As a human being, once you allow the shadow walker to connect or attach to your human body or soul, you begin to transform into its supernatural demonic (trans) ways. Now you are a part of their world call the fire of hell. The shadow walker actually walks among us on the face of this earth using many identities. If you are not careful, you can be pulled into its world by your eyes being covered by not seeing the shadow walker of its identity.

God is about truth and honesty. God does not have to deceive you into doing his will. God gives us the opportunity to make our own choices (good or evil). On that note, I choose good over evil anytime. It is the acceptance of wanting to see the beaming light, not the dark clouds that can be folded before us. In this world, he has dominion and power over all things as the creator. God says good can overcome evil as long as you stay connected to his will. The Bible states that in Roman 12:21, "Do not be overcome by evil but overcome evil with good. There is only one way that evil can overcome a Christian, and that is if a Christian returns evil for evil." God gives us dominion and power to rule over these things. We have power over these things here on earth.

However, whether the adversaries (evil) come up against you using any or many tactics, you cannot be defeated because of the Christ in you. The light that is in you can overcome the shadow of the darkness. So, sister and brother, we have to be in the will of God to recognize and acknowledge his glory. So I beseech you, sister and brother, to take off those sunglasses or the 3D glasses that have created an illusion to your view. It can put you into a dimension of unreality.

In the Bible, John 8:12 states that Jesus spoke to the people once more and said, "I am the light of the world. If you follow me, you will not have to walk in darkness because you will have the light that leads to life."

So, sister and brother, we have to be in the will of God to recognize and acknowledge his glory. So I beseech you, sister and brother, to take off those dark sunglasses from your eyes that protect you from seeing the sunlight and the world from what it really is, hidden your emotions and your insecurities. It does not show your identity (anonymous). It is said that another dimension to sunglasses is their ability to promote the illusion of having a baby's face (double-sided face). We do not know whether you're old or young (pretending or perpetrating). There is no realness about you at all; it throws off your character. It is said that the eyes truly are the windows to the soul, so hiding your eyes can potentially hide a lot. We could not live life fully if we were hiding behind our sunglasses or the 3D glasses.

The 3D glasses can also take effect on creating an illusion to your view. It can put you into a dimension of unreality (a false idea or belief). It is an object or thing that is or likely to be wrongly perceived or interpreted by the senses (sight, smell, hearing, taste, and touch). It is an unreal or misleading appearance or image. Its definition is explained by in order to see the content in 3D; the brain needs to be tricked into making it believe it sees something in 3D (fake) that is actually only 2D (regular flat screen).

This is the same operation of the enemy, the unrevealing shadow walker, who comes to play tricks with your mind and cloud your eyes as if you were wearing 3D glasses. The shadow walker will have you believe you are in a fantasy world. The fantasy world that the enemy had helped to create, through your own pleasant/pleasure situation that you enjoy thinking about, but it was unlikely to happen. It will (shadow walker) have you filled with excitement and thrill by playing a role in his scenes. The shadow walker job is to play its role in being cunning, sneaky, outwit someone, a scheme intended to deceive, skill act, mislead, delude, double-cross, swindle, hoax, bamboozle, fool, pull the wool over someone eyes, or con.

The 2D refers to objects or images that show only two dimensions (horizontal and vertical) which can only be portrayed in images and art (it has no layers, no depths, no effects, no extra dimensions, plain flat surface, no shadow, and it's a plain look). It has no visual effects like in the 3D when you are wearing the 3D glasses. It just like watching on your screen with surround sound. It actually sees the same thing in each eye (a single view of a clear reality of a 2D, no double effects).

The 3D refers to those that show three dimensions (layers, shadows, curves, edges, or objects coming out of the screen), which occurs by sending different images in each of the eyes (spirits that work like a transmitter who transmit electromagnetic waves carrying messages or signals, especially those of radio, television, or movie screens, etc.) of the members of the audience (observer, crowd, or viewer). It can give the viewer a creative image of imitating (fake, duplicate, pretend, or mimic) the appearance or character of. It is a motion picture that enhances the illusion and brings you into the reality of the screen. The effect is enough to deceive the brain.

It is also said that 3D imaging or the art of stereoscopy refers to a technique for creating or enhancing the illusion of depth in an image by presenting two offset images separately to your left and right eyes. Your brain then combines the two visuals to create a single 3D image of the objects. If both eyes see both visuals, then the brain will not be able to create a 3D image of the object but will create a 2D blurred, out of focus image only, often referred to as ghostly.

The spirits can transform through many telecommunications devices, whether it is all types of voices, data, and video transmissions. The spirits of a shadow walker are like a disease transmission when an infection passes from one living thing onto another. God transmission is used through speaking to a man of righteousness. God communicates his word to man (apostles, prophetess, or prophets) as a living soul.

Our God is a speaking God (Hebrews 1:1–2). It is said that the transmission of the Holy Bible is the process by which man obtained, preserved, and passed on God's speaking through times. God telecommunicates through. 2 Timothy 3:16 says, "All scripture is God breathed and profitable for teaching, for conviction, for correction, for instruction in righteousness." Also, the Word says, "The words which I have spoken to you are spirit and are life" John 6:63b.

However, sister and brother, we want to feel the true greatness of our God and God's reality. We just need a touch of God's anointed power to clear our view. Once our view is clear, we can experience that amazing view of God's sunshine.

So, sister and brother, do not allow the unrevealing shadow walker to take control, operate, and blind our eyes. God wants the best for us, and he truly cares. So wake up and uncover your eyes and see the true relationship that you are in or coming at you from different angles.

People, uncover your eyes and receive the true blessing which God has for you. God's gift is unique, loving, kind, and happy. God does not cause pain and hurt. Our God truly knows the best for us when putting a relationship together that he designs. Always remember, people, that he is the one who has made us, not we ourselves. So why allow your eyes to be covered by the darkness of the unrevealing shadow walker who comes to deceive you from seeing the real reality of God's blessings. God cannot bless you if the unrevealing shadow walker is still standing in your view. The shadow walker is one who walks the line between light and darkness. It is one that does not choose a side between dark and light. They walk the gray path. It is not real, and it does not have any stability. The shadow walker understands that human activities can be monitored and tracked by modern technology, but because of many diverse interests and activities, the unrevealing shadow walker strives to keep his or her real identity below the radar. However, they are more vulnerable in bright sunlight.

Listen, you have to choose between light and darkness. You do not want to live in darkness because it serves you no good, so why not consider light, which causes you to have peace, joy, love, happiness, and eternal life. The Bible states that Jesus is the light of the world: "whoever follows me will never walk in darkness but shall have the light of life" (John 8:12). In a relationship, you want someone that has stability which is being stable, steadiness, endurance, maturity, communication and balance. These are all good things that represent the love of God. The darkness is sadness, cold, loneliness, something you cannot love, and its gloom.

However, if you do not open your eyes, it will keep you into its darkness. This is not the type of relationship that God ordained for a man or woman to live in darkness, especially if it's an unbalanced one of violence, lies, cheating, saying hurtful words (verbal abuse), being controlling, emotionally abusive, jealousy, unrealistic expectation, isolation, or sudden mood swings. These are the signs of an unrevealed shadow walker who lurks somewhere between light and darkness and life and death. It waits or moves in a secret way so that it cannot be seen, especially because if it is about to attack someone or do something wrong. It is an unpleasant feeling or quality to exist, although it is not always noticeable. The shadow walker forms in many identities. Such as, it can form in the shadow of your own identity, like the reflection of the production of an image by or if by a mirror. Also, it can walk on the face of the earth by attaching itself to one human body. People, if you are blinded by the unrevealing shadow walker, you do not know who you are coming up against because perpetrators (deception) are real. It can have you thinking that they are truly in love with you for you, support you, and even have you flipping the script as if you were all about them. You would not even believe that your own mind is being controlled.

God's gift is genuine, and it is a satisfaction to your soul. The man above will not bless you with something or anything that is not right in the spirit anyway, especially if it does not have your name on it. As a man or woman, we tend to force our name on something or anything because we desire it, seek after it, hunger after it, admire it, or lust after it. Then we fall for it right into the devil's trap. This is nothing but the unrevealing shadow walker who came along to deceive you into having those unclean feelings. Listen very carefully: if anything that does not come into the light and always stay in the dark or in between the light or the dark, it is being deceitful (*the walking shadow or walking corpse*). This is because it does not want to be uncovered or disposed to show its true in and out appearance (true colors). Before you know it, you will be walking in the flesh as a dead corpse or zombie. What's dead, let it stay dead and buried from around your territory (unclean spirit), and what's alive, let it stay alive and well in the freshness of our maker, our Lord or King (righteousness spirit).

Chapter 5

THE DEVIL FICTION (IMAGINATION/FALSELY) VERSUS GOD'S NONFICTION (FACTS/TRUTH)

You can find the unrevealing shadow walker identity by its aroma. Its aroma scents off like a bad-smelling disease or corpse (a foul smell). If you are in the will of God, you can detect it by its aroma. No matter how it changes clothing, it will give off its identity by this unpleasant aroma. In the Bible, 2 Corinthians 2:16 states, "To the one we are an aroma that brings death (Savior of death); to the other, an aroma that brings life (Savior of life). And who is equal to such task?"

To the men and women, you have to remember that it comes in many forms and fashion. It can look like you, sound like you, act like you, smell like you, eat like you, and dress like you. It is full of lies, garbage, and trash (the blood of Jesus and the devil is a liar). It does not mean you any good; it is dead and rotten. The enemy's job is to come and defile you. The shadow walker is contaminated. It can make you befoul your own house. A sinful thing does not please God on his camping grounds. This is why you have to be in place of God's will to see right through the enemy's deceitful ways. Therefore, it is not worthy of holding on to that person if God did not allow it. When you want something so bad, God will say you got just what you wanted because you are mesmerized by what you see and hear of your own taste of desire.

You were not able to think about anything else that includes God. You were put into a trance by the enemy. Then you get caught up in saying "I do" down to the altar with a double personality, hidden agenda, or face trick of the scheme (3D glasses on) the shadow walker.

Listen, men and women of God, I am not telling you to move them away or out if God says it is your destiny to go through the storm or your battle (marriage). God won't give us anything that we cannot handle because we can survive through staying in the will of God. If God tells us to end the relationship, step away and do not engage yourself in a marriage. We have to follow his will on our lives in obedience. However, let God work on that individual soul, but you stand back and be still. This means God is warning us before destruction hits our life. God gives everyone a task of their very own battle to face. He will not give us anything that we cannot bear or handle. You have to really be in place of God to see and hear what is good and what is not good, when to stay and when to go when to separate or to stay joined when to fight with words of righteousness or when to fall back and let God handle the task. Your task is what the love of God wants it to be in his will and not your own will. Everybody's storms are different. What works for one may not work for you. God gives everyone instructions to the fullness of how to deal with your hurt and pain. God cares truly about your well-being. Sometimes God will take the worst and messed-up creature and turn it into something good (for his glory and your glory). God attends it to be before us, but we ourselves cannot change or fix up that individual on our own. God's love and prayer can conquer anything. God comes on the battleground/field and fights for his children when we let him and stand back to see the process perform (manifestation).

However, as men and women, we tend to believe what we want to see as our own design, man or woman, for our life partner. In reality, he or she is not the one God designed for us because we were so fascinated and blinded by the untruth. I have learned from a pastor that if you were not told or did not seek God for approval in getting married, and you have been living in an abomination, that was not pleasing to God. You have set your own self up for destruction because you took it upon yourself to do things your own way without God's approval. I took it upon myself to get married because I did not want to live in sin, and I truly loved him. I wanted to make it right for my household, and I did not want to keep living in sin with a man. I went ahead and got married without God's approval, and I ended up facing a lot of hard aches and disappointments. When we go ahead without God's will, we face our own after. God knows the future into any matter of our lives. God knows better for our life because he sees what we will be facing, good or evil. I cold blinded my own destiny. I asked God to please forgive me for stepping ahead of him.

As the Word says, the truth shall set you free. There's a song that says, "I once was lost but now I'm found. I once was blind but now I see. But we still are lost, and we still do not see," because we still fall short of his glory by not trusting God. This is because, as men and women, we tend to hold on for the simple fact that we try very hard to fix it, make it right, clean it up, or make it seem like in our imaginary mind that it's going to get better, or you may even say to yourself to let nature take its course, it will eventually work out on its own. But it never will, or it never does get better because we attend to step one foot ahead of God. The Bible says in Psalm 37:23, "The steps of a good man are ordered by the Lord: and he delighteth in his way."

I want to encourage you with this word Isaiah 40:21, "Surely you know, surely you have heard, surely from the beginning someone told you, surely you understand how the earth was created." Because he is perfect, all-powerful, and knows everything. God transcended nature mysteriously though he still concerns himself with our life. God is always first, and God will surely be last. He says that he is the alpha and omega, the beginning, and the ending, the first and the last. For he had said, "He will never leave thee nor forsake thee" at any times (Deuteronomy 31:6). God just wants the best for us because he loves us with the utmost. Just let go and let God. (Try him out for yourself; he will never let you down by any means necessary.) He will never abandon his mission when it comes to fighting your battles. He got your back even when others have failed you and bailed out. God stands beside you until victory has been won. You may have stepped out the will of God in marring or been put in a bad relationship when God may have said wait or not that one. The one thing about our King, he will still come to our rescue when we repent and cry out to his will. He is our fixer-upper who comes to restore us in the sound of a heartbeat.

The Lord has all the tools he needs to accommodate us for what we need. Why do we need to mix and match up to our own mate? Sometimes we even go on to dating websites to look for our ideal person. Proverbs 18:22 states, "He who finds a wife finds a good thing and obtain favor for the Lord." You are completely taking over God's job. God sees beyond every person's life. God knows all things. We do not need to solve the problem ourselves like we are the fixer-upper. Especially when we have the attendances to hear, seek advice, and get approval from our family or relatives or close friends with whom we are dating or in a relationship. We must be very careful of seeking the advice of someone else's ideas or beliefs is and (reliable) trusted approval because it will and can cause disaster or failure. You can depend on God's thoughts and trusted approval; it is the best advice to anyone. We should just focus on fixing ourselves on life, in having a great relationship with God. Just take the time out to seek what God has to say first about the person with who you are involved, dating, or in a relationship.

Proverbs 16:1 and 7 says, "We can make our own plans, but the Lord gives the right answer… We can make our own plans, but the Lord determines our steps." Meanwhile, people, you do not have to settle for the mess. So clean it up and settle for the best.

Our God does warn us in many ways either by dreams, through the Bible, through people or friends, sometimes using signs, using circumstances, or just saying yes. God lets us know that the relationships or any other situation you are in won't work or it is not for you. God does give plenty of signs to show us how we must live in this world. In the Bible, Proverbs 16:18 says, "Pride goeth before destruction, and a haughty spirit before it falls or the destructive pride brings down many winners and is contagious." It does say warning comes before destruction, especially when you lose focus on God of not seeing or hearing his voice or signs. Sometimes we tend to look past the signs and ignore the truth for what it is. The whole purpose of the warning is to prevent what will take place in your life. God's warning is sent to protect us, not punish us. God does look out for our future. However, I am a witness to the signs and wonders, and I am so glad I am in the process of learning to obey God's will. I fell short lots of time, but I admitted to my faults, and I strive to have a determination to make it right as well as get it right. No one in this world is a cup of cream and sugar. Sometimes people have fallen short in letting their cream and sugar become sour and bitter (unsweet) at some point in their life. We slip and fall, but we can stand steady. We are not perfect, but we can strive to make it better for ourselves (staying humble in the will of God). You are a conqueror, and you can make it. Please remember you can win by the grace of the almighty King. You are on the winning side of God, which can be your season of walking out as victories. I had a praying mother, family, friends, and church folks who help me through my trial and tribulations and still are praying for and encouraging my soul.

This is where the unrevealing shadow walker plays its role by manipulating the mind of a human being. The shadow walker is a spirit that dwells around your presents secretly. It trails, watches, keeps in sight, and pursues. Once the shadow walker comes in your present, it will come against your mind, body, and soul by operating itself into a human being (if you allow it). The shadow walker is like a shadow box that is an imaginary opponent in training (to box or fight) with one's shadow. (The shadow walker is trained to fight against your flesh or weakness to take you down and control your soul.) The shadow walker will hit you with all different unclean punches against your body. (It does not play fair at all.) It is ready to defeat you and knock you off your balance (transforms itself on your shadow). God will teach or condition you how to take a body shot or punch against the shadow walker. The shadow walkers show us things that we desire as if you are living in a reality show or paradise. The shadow walkers can form into many personalities/masks, for instance:

1. the desires (fantasies)

2. the seeker (finding human flesh to be used)

3. the hunger (hunger after your soul, a strong or eager desire or longing for or craving)

4. the admirer (eye contact of interest of wrongful thoughts)

5. the lust(er) (the fulfilling/consumed of a very strong sexual desires of their own personal needs)

Here, I will walk you through my past relationships, marriage, circumstances, and the process of healing through faith. You will see from the definition of an unrevealing shadow walker how it operates through the human being. You will see an example of the shadow walker who has worn many hats.

Chapter 6

MY JOURNEY THROUGH RELATIONSHIPS, MARRIAGE, TRAP, HEALING, FORGIVING, TRUSTING, AND HOPE MY SOUL SALVATION

The First Relationship

I went through a lot of bad relationships. For example, I can remember when I was a senior in high school. I went out on a date with this young man. He came to the house and introduced himself to my mother. After they were introduced, my mother asked to see his driver's license. She wanted to make sure he was not bad news, making sure his identification was accurate. My mother was very much protective of her children. Also, my mother made it very clear to the young man to make sure "you bring my daughter back at a decent time and no funny business," if you know what I mean. Then my mother pulled me to the side and asked if I had money in my pocket. There were also pagers and beepers back in the day as well. My mother always said not to trust no one and always keep a phone on me and money in my pocket just in case something goes wrong.

The young man and I proceeded out the door to our date. He took me out to eat and introduced me to a couple of his friends. Then he took me to his house, and I met his mother. After that, we watched television in the living room. Then he said, Let us go downstairs to my room." We went downstairs, and he showed me around his room. He had a lot of trophies. He was into sports. Soon as I sat down on his couch, he decided he wanted to get his grove on. He did not waste any time. I was very uncomfortable.

Then I said the word no, and he did not like it. The young boy was upset and said, "Okay, I am going to take you home." Notice how I said boy and not man because he acts in a childish way of immaturity. A real man would have respected your wishes and continued in an adult manner. I did not say a word. I just kept thinking like, Wow, my mother told me about guys like this. Then I said, "Please, God, just get me home." The young boy took me home really quickly by speeding. Then he dropped me off to the curve and kept it moving. I was a little surprised but not upset at all. I just was not that type of girl. He was not the one for me. He showed his true colors, and God allowed me to see it for what it was (dead beat). I just thank God it did not turn into something worse. God was watching over my life. Thank God for my mama and church friends for having a close relationship with God. The mask/personality of this shadow walker showed itself by oozing his charm on my mother and me. When he did not get what he wanted, he put me out onto the curve and kept it moving. I never heard or seen him again after that date night. He was finished with me because I did not give in to what he wanted (the spirit of a player). This player (unrevealing shadow walker) gave me a 3D illusion (pretending to be kindhearted, flashing his nice car, and being a sports player) of being accompanied by a decent and respectable man. He was a true con artist. I am so glad the 3D illusions did not entrap me completely. It came out of its shadow box when I said the word no. I did not give in and give him what he wanted.

The Second Relationship

However, I can also remember other incidents that I went through while I was in a relationship. I met a guy whose cousin was dating my sister. He came over to the house for the first time. He was so good looking, tall, and chocolate. I started blushing, but I was very shy. I never really had a real date or even been in a relationship at all. I was really new at this stuff, and I never had sex. I was a quiet person. Soon, I started going to his house, and he came over to my house frequently. Then I assumed we were dating. However, back then, as I look at it now, I did not know what kind of relationship that was. Because we never went on a date, like to the movies, go out to eat, or even go shopping together. I thought that was how it was supposed to be, just going back and forth to each other's house.

Listen, people, I was so naive. I have never, as I said before, been with a guy before. As I went a couple of times to his house, I met his grandparents, uncles, father, and cousin, who lived upstairs from his grandparent's home. They were so nice to me and loveable. They made sure I had something to drink and offered me dinner. I really enjoyed coming over because I felt comfortable.

Soon, things began to change once I felt very comfortable with this guy.

However, the guy I was seeing had his own space downstairs in the basement of his grandparents' home. It was like another apartment. I was so in love with him. I thought he was so fine looking, and you could not tell me anything. Soon, things started to change for the worse. When he called me to come over to his house to chill that night, I had no idea that my life was about to change. That night was when I was no longer a virgin. I let my guard down because my heart was in love for the first time. We started having sex a lot. I did not mind because he was my first. I loved and trusted him. When you are inexperienced and do not know much about relationships, you can sign up into some deep mess. I can remember one night, my mother cooked dinner. My mother and her closest friend were sitting at the kitchen table. I came into the kitchen and asked what was for dinner, and my mother said chicken and rice. I went over to the stove, took the lid off, and grabbed a spoon. Then I started eating inside that big pot. Suddenly out of nowhere, I was extremely hungry. I could not stop eating at all out of the big pot.

My mother said, "Girl, why are you eating over that pot like that? Get a plate and sit down and eat." Then she said, "Why your butt looks like it's spread wide." Then my mother's closest friend looked at me and said, "Your neck has two heartbeats." I said, "What does that mean? I never heard of that before." My mother said, "I do not know, Cathy. Your butt is spreading, your breast looks big, and you are eating like crazy over the pot." The next day, my mother took me to the doctor for a checkup. I will never forget the African American male doctor that examined me. He was so nice and patient. My mother did all the talking. Then the doctor asked me about my last period and how I felt. The doctor then had me lay down onto the table and put his hand on my lower stomach. The doctor looked at me, my mother, and said, "She is pregnant." Then the doctor took bloodwork and asked me to come back in a couple of days to confirm. When I went back to the doctor, he confirmed my pregnancy and how far along I was. I left the doctor's office and exited out the front entrance. I then stood outside by the door and looked up toward the sky. I took a long breath and thought, God, is this real? Then I looked down at my stomach and placed my hand on it and said, "It is going to be okay. I will be there for you." I did not feel scared or nervous at that very moment.

I went home and confirmed the pregnancy with my mother.

My mother said before all this, she had a dream about a fish, and when she looked at me in the kitchen that night, it was confirmed. My mother said, "You are going to have to let him know about the pregnancy." Eventually, I called my boyfriend and told him about me being pregnant. He really did not have too much to say. He then had a cab to come and get me. I arrived at his house and came in, and then I went downstairs to the basement. As I went in, I walked toward the bar and sat on the stool. Then my boyfriend, at that time, said a few words. So I went to pick up the remote control to turn the channel. Suddenly, he looked at me and said, "Don't be getting too comfortable in here, changing channel like you got like that." So I got up and went over to the couch and sat down. I was speechless. It was all because I was pregnant. I really was not a talkative person. I just watch, listen mostly, and laugh a lot. Soon things started to change for the worse.

I remember I went home and went about my usual day. A couple of days later, his mother called, and my mother answered the phone. His mother stated to my mother that my son does not think he is the father, and I was lying around with other guys. Boy, oh, boy, my mother went off. She told her, "Your son needs to grow up. My daughter was a virgin when she got involved with your son. She doesn't lie around with other guys. He's a liar, and you need to teach your son responsibilities and respect." I was so hurt by this and started crying a lot. As days went by, I noticed how I was not getting any phone calls from my boyfriend at all. I eventually made a phone call to him, and he asked me to come over to his house so we can talk. When I arrived, he did not look too pleasant, like he had something heavy on his mind. He eventually started talking. He wanted me to get an abortion, and he was going to pay for the abortion. I just listened and started to agree, but my mind and heart were saying something different.

He started having me come to his house more often, and he was coming to my house. He was still getting sex from me like he had no care in the world. He was trying to repeatedly talk me into getting an abortion. I really did not understand because the whole time he was trying to talk me into having an abortion, he was having sex with me at the same time. It made me feel helpless, used, and terrible, especially because I allowed him to have sex with me even through my pain. I really loved this man, even in his selfishness. The only time I would see him is when he wanted to talk about abortion. I was so in the dark, wearing my 3D glasses of allowing this man to take advantage of my heart.

I remember one night, my mother came into my room because I was crying so much. My mother said out of the kindness of her heart, "Whatever choice you make, I will still be there for you. Whether you choose to get an abortion or keep the baby, it's still your choice, but you know I raised you better than that, and I don't believe in abortion and that's a sin." I eventually told him that I was keeping the baby. Soon as I said I was keeping my baby, things started to change even more. There were no more phone calls and visits from him at all. I was on my own carrying this heavy load of not knowing what to do. I was scared, nervous, alone, hurt, and disappointed by this man leaving me alone to handle this by myself. How ungrateful this man is for bailing out.

I started crying even more until my mother came to me again and said, "Stop crying. It's not good for the baby. You're not alone because you have me and God to see you through this." So I pulled myself together and started getting help (public assistance) for me and the baby. I called the father because my mother said I need to get more help and not let him get away with not taking responsibility. He agreed sending me money to help, but when he started sending me money, I could not believe how much it was—$15, $20, or $35. Sometimes, I did not even see any money for weeks. My mother told me not to worry again. God is going to deal with him. I went to the store with my brother's girlfriend who was pregnant as well. We saw him walking down the street with another girl, and he walked by me as if I was nothing but a stranger on the street. My brother's girlfriend looked at him and went off. She started cursing and saying, "How you going to walk by the person that is caring your child and do not say nothing." It was so hurtful because the girl he was seeing lived right around the corner from where I lived. He was not with me throughout the whole pregnancy, and he did not even come to the hospital when I delivered my son. My mother was there with me the whole time in the delivery room. I was way overdue and had difficulty in delivering my beautiful, precious son. My mother called for the entire prayer warriors to come together and pray. The doctor did not know what was going on with me. They said I was losing oxygen and the baby's heartbeat was going up and down and they did not know why. The doctor even told my mother they may have to give me blood transfusion and she needed to sign paper just in case. My mother said, "No, I am not going to sign that because I do not want the hospital to use their blood." She told them I have the same blood type as my father. My father was on standby at his house just in case they needed him, but he never came to the hospital to even visit. I was given an oxygen mask to receive air. I did not really use it because it did not seem to help at all. I just tossed it away.

The doctors still did not know why my baby was having trouble coming out. So they had to call in for the specialist, the head doctor. I remember when she came into my room—a black African American woman doctor. She was very cheerful. She said, "You guys got me out here in all this heavy rain and thunder. It's time for you to come out, little one." Then she smiled at me and said, "You and the baby is going to be fine. Let us see what the problem is." They moved me from the regular room into the delivery room. The head doctor put her hands in me. Then the baby was coming, and she quickly told me to stop pushing. The cord was wrapped around my baby's neck and face. If I would have pushed, he would have died right there in the delivery room. The head doctor had to quickly turn my baby around so that she could untangle him from my cord. I was in the hospital for two days trying to deliver my baby. He came out by the grace of the almighty God, my mother, and the prayer warriors. He was so handsome with a lot of hair and sucking loud on his hands (he had swelling around his eyes). The doctor said, "Somebody is hungry." My mother said, "I would be hungry being in the room for two days and no food to eat." I really thank God for bringing my baby boy safely out of my womb and all the doctors who played their part in helping to deliver my baby.

My son's father never took the opportunity to be there to experience the whole pregnancy up to my son being born. God, my mother, the prayer warriors, and the doctors get the full credit.

After I had my son, we were seeing each other again, but he still was not right. I did not completely let go. I was still holding on to filth (the deceitful unrevealing shadow walker). I remember when I was working, he would come by my job, which was a daycare center I was working at, to pick up our son. He would drop him off to his house, and we would have talks and be intimate with each other at my house. I can also remember one night, I was talking to him about how I feel, and I wanted more (marriage). I really loved him a whole

lot. He was agreeing and was respecting how I felt at that time, or so I thought. He was just agreeing so that he can have sex with me.

One day, I was at the job. It was a Friday. He called me to pick up our son. He came to get him, and then I asked if he was keeping him for the weekend. He said yes. I also asked if he was coming to my house to pick up some clothes for him. He said he did not need to do that. He will drop him off that Sunday. I thought that was odd and strange at first because he never would have said he did not need some clothes from our son. He normally would tell me to make sure I pack some clothes or he will pick them up later that night. He came over anyway to be with me while our son was at his house with the grandparents. We talked and laughed. Then I noticed how he kept getting quiet, and I asked if everything was okay because it seemed like he was carrying something heavy on his mind. He said no, that everything was fine. He helped wash my hair and greased my scalped that night. Then we became intimate with each other that night.

Meanwhile, that next day, which was a Saturday, my mother and I were at home. My mother came to me that day and said one of the church members called her concerning my son. She was rapping about how handsome he looked outside in front of a church wearing a white tuxedo with a dark-skinned man who also wore a white tuxedo. My mother said, "You saw my grandson?" The church member said, "Yes, I was driving past and seen your grandson and this man out in front of the church." The church member asked who was getting married. My mother asked me, "Who do you know is getting married?" I said, "I do not know because his father would have told me about it." My mother said, "That is not your son's father getting married?" I said, "No, not at all." In my mind, we just had our talk about this and we've been intimate with each other. We are in a relationship as I thought, otherwise from seeing each other particularly almost every night.

I decided to call to find out what is going on. When I called, the grandfather picked up, and he did not sound too good. I asked him how he felt. He said he was not feeling good and his wife had gone on to the church for my son's father's wedding. I said, "I am sorry, what did you say?" He said, "Yes, Tee is getting married today."

I froze and my mother said, "What is wrong with you?" I told the grandfather, "I hope you feel better and take care," and I hung up the phone. I told my mother what we talked about, which was my son's father was getting married. I could not believe what I heard. I yelled and screamed. We have been with each other for a while. But what I could not get out of my head was we were sexually involved, especially that Friday, and the next day, he jumped up and got married. My god, how totally wrong was to lay with a woman and get married the next day to another woman. I remember my son used to tell me his dad would take him over to a lady's house all the time and would cook and have dinner with her. But when confronted, his father denied it or said that my son didn't know what he was talking about. I asked him that Friday night if everything was okay, and he said yes. I knew something was wrong when he was acting a little different that night. He had the whole opportunity to talk about it, but he chose not to because he wanted his cake and eats it as well.

I want to let you know that even when he hurt me by getting married, he tried to make an excuse by saying he married her because she was pregnant and that his grandparents said he should marry her because he didn't need to have kids all over the place and he needed to settle down. I in turn said, "What do you mean? I thought people should marry for love, not to have other reasons." I also said, "What about me? I got pregnant and had your child. Why didn't I get that opportunity of being married?" I was yelling and crying, saying, "You are wrong! You are not going to get away with it. Stay away from me, you jerk!" He was involved with two women at the same time. He was working through his body like a three-dimensional character in a real world. His character performed in a pair of conflicting emotions. He set himself to be believable, he had flaws and failing, he was an individual who sought to relate to others, and he had his own story, irrational, quirky, often social. The three dimensions in a character are spirit, soul, and body or mental, physical, and emotional.

I was angry, and I have not heard from him in about a week or two. He knew he did wrong by me and my son. Eventually, he was trying to ease back around again, especially because we have a son together so that was his excuse. You would think one would learn from all this, but I got caught up again because he would stay more at my house and then his own. My dad would say to my mom, "Why is he always over my daughter's house all the time? Isn't he married, and why he married the other girl anyway? My daughter looks better than her." My mother said, "James, leave it alone. She is grown."

However, I knew the ball game was in my hands. I could do whatever I wanted, get whatever I wanted, and however I wanted. I started to grow more anger because in my mind, I wanted to get back at him totally. Deep down I was still in love with this man. I became the deceitful shadow walker because of hurt and pain. I allowed my hurt and pain to turn into revenge. I wanted to make that person feel trapped into his own mess. He will come over so much as if he lived with me. I would say, "You are a married man, and you are over my house like this." His response was, "Let me worry about it. I am a grown man. I know what I am doing, and I will face my own consequences." My response was, "You do not feel any remorse because I feel like I am in the middle of this problem." I also said, "This is not right at all."

One day, when he came over, we were sitting on the couch talking, and he got up and went to the bathroom. I took the phone and called his house. I asked to speak to him, and his wife would say he was not here. I said, "Okay, tell him I called, and he is upstairs using the rest room." I would laugh about it because I did not care. I was still hurting. My son's father would come over to the house to pick up my son and leave him with his wife, then come back to my house and chill. Sometimes when he came over, he would come on to me, and I would push him, run out from the room, and repeatedly tell him to stop. I would be in the bathroom taking a bath, and he'd be trying to come in and he would be at the door, saying, "Let me in the bathroom." I would say, "No, wait until I get out."

He'd give me money, pay my bills, buy me things, and if I see something I like, he'd give me money to buy it. This was besides the money I was receiving from child support. But one thing I did not like was when he'd give me money or if I asked for money for emergency, he'd take advantage of it by wanting to have sex before he gave me the money. Then afterward he'd tell me he only has this amount or I should let him know ahead of time on his pay period. I would feel used because I felt like I had to pay for it by having sex. I realized that when he came over one night to bring me money to take care of the light bill. I asked him if he had the money. He said yes (liar). I asked for the money, and he said, "Wait, I will give it to you. There is no rush." He stayed over late, and we were intimate or active with each other. When he got ready to leave, he said, "I only have $50." I asked for $100. He said, "You got to catch me on my payday." When you think you got control of something, which was unclean in the first place, the tables always turn around and bite you back.

It was like that with him. If he must give me money or anything, I had to pay for it through sex. The sad thing about it was I did not even get what I asked for half the time. It was like I was a prostitute and not the mother of his child. I would feel all this in my heart, but I would not say anything. I just let him do whatever and however. He had control again. Darn it. I was trying to hold on to a man that was not any good from the front door at all (a married man). I was in love but still hurting. He had a hold on my life.

I was so wrong for accepting him back in my life, especially because he was a married man now. Two wrongs do not make it right. I really let my guard down because in my heart, I was still in love with him, but he's a married man. He kept telling me he made a mistake and he was in love with me. In my heart, I know this was wrong, and I had to let it go. I kept thinking that I was cheating myself out of life. God is not pleased with this type of lifestyle. I realized that I could not do this anymore and I was wasting time and energy in an unhealthy relationship that was not going anywhere. Sometimes, we can be so caught up in giving our hearts to someone that we will literally allow that man to have control over us and waste time and years. Once I made up my mind to stand strong, mean business, and give it up, I was a free woman. I realized I was not gaining anything from this unclean relationship. I allowed the enemy to settle revenge in my heart and got bitten back because the tables turned back on me. I fell into the trap of the shadow walker of my own combat. I was doing evil for evil.

When I decided to break it off, it did not go so well. He came over my house that morning or evening. I decided to tell him I met someone else, and I was beginning to like him a lot. Why did I mention that? He grabbed me and pushed me up against the kitchen sink. I was totally in shock. He was really upset because I wanted to let it go and move on. I did not understand because he had someone, his wife, and I wanted more. He was not able to give me what I wanted—a healthy relationship, and I was tired of hearing excuses and babies popping up in the midst of it all. I called my best friend Lakeisha on the same day, and she said, "Girl, you never break up with a man in person. You do it over the phone just to prevent things like that for having physical contact. A man does not want to hear your breaking up with them." I said I did not think nothing of it because he's married. She said, "It does not matter. You're involved in a relationship with him in his eyes." I said, "He caught himself and went out the door."

For instance (record check), his wife has a home; I have an apartment. She has a truck and a car; I have a car and still making payments on it. She has a husband that has an excellent job and takes care of all her financial needs; I'm still a single working mother still getting help from different organizations to help with my financial needs. She gets to go on vacation and trip, and I get to vacation at home or over a friend's house and no trips unless the job is sending a group of us on a teacher convention. I also got to hear that she was having babies after babies, and I just sat back and listened to the sob stories I was supposed to accept. It did not belong to me because it belongs to someone else now. My name was not on the marriage certificate; it had someone else's name on it. He did not even think I was worthy to put a ring on it because he thought of someone else's ring finger. I was not worth the dignity to earn or have my name on a marriage certificate. I did not want to be second for anybody. When we were in a relationship from the beginning, he never knew my favorite color, the music I like, the flower I like, what I like to do, or what was my goals for the future. He was just a person that used and bruised the heart of a good woman. I had to ask God for forgiveness and forgave myself. This was not worth it at all, and this surely was not love at all. I went through so much with my son's father, but I took charge over my life. There is someone that God has for me and for you as well. It does not matter how long it takes (months, years, or weeks) for God to send that special one into your life. You may have gone through a lot of trials and tribulation in a dysfunctional relationship, but know that the best solution is to step aside and wait on your prince and queen. Sometimes waiting and being patience is the best result that anyone can gain in life.

I went through so many tests and trials, but God still covered me. God does send warnings for our safety. This shadow walker (mask/personality) was oozing charms, taking advantage of every good thing he learned from me, turning his back on me, showering me with gifts and money. I confide in him about my work, family life, and most aspects of my life. I trusted him.

My first true love gave me a 3D illusion into a world of a make-believe showcase. He made me feel comfortable, wanted, trusting, loved, and caring. He gave me the impression that he was truly the one for me, that there was not going to be no other before me or after me. Nevertheless, it was just an illusion of the shadow walker being a pretender and a liar. He showed his true colors of being selfish, inconsiderate, not supportive, bailing out, unworthy, and conniving. I was nervous, emotional, alone, helpless, used, felt terrible, hurt, and disappointed of this inhuman being of a man. My sisters and brothers, when the enemy knows your profile, you can believe you're being setup for entrapment.

Note: Revenge is not the key to solving the solution to ease your pain. It only makes it worse for yourself and others who are involved. The unrevealing shadow walker can make you feel high (like on cloud nine or jolly green giant) just to bring you down and feel like nothing. However, true love does not hurt you, deceive you, or play tricks with your emotions.

The Third Relationship

I can contest to another relationship that I was in that I will never forget. God's grace and mercy stood by my side again. I had another beautiful handsome son by a man that was very deceitful (false face). We met through my brother when he was locked up in Annandale Prison. My brother would call home to speak to my mother a lot. My brother would talk to my mother about a friend he had that was locked up with him and said that he looked out for him in buying him food and putting money into his account. My mother was not happy nor pleased with this at all. She made sure my brother had everything he needed and made food to bring down to him on visitation. I remember my mother asked my brother, "Why is he being so nice and always giving you things?" She would say, "I do not know about this, James. If you okay with it, then fine." My brother was really concerned about my mother because he knew her struggles, and he did not want to put more burdens on her especially when it was his mistake.

My brother and his friend were talking to my mother on several occasions, and he started to call her mom. Then my brother put me on the phone with his friend, and we chatted several times. I was not really feeling him at all. I was just being nice and carrying a friendly conversation. However, I had forgotten about him until one day he called my house and stated who he was and said he has been home for a month. He wanted to know if he can take me out. I said yes because I did not have anything to do. He eventually came and picked me up in his car. We went out to eat, and then he took me to meet his son who he lived in Lakewood, New Jersey. I met his son, sisters, uncle, mother, and grandmother. Wow! I cannot believe this all happened in one day. The family was very nice to me. We started hanging out a lot, meeting more of his family and friends. Then he would buy me jewelry and clothes and bring it to my job to surprise me. One day, he took me to meet his oldest sister and her kids, and he had introduced me as his girlfriend. I was not feeling this at all because I did not agree being his girlfriend. When we got into his car, I approached him about his announcement. I said, "When was I supposed to know that I was your girlfriend? You did not ask me at all." He said, "I thought since we have been going out a lot, it's okay." I said, "Nothing is okay if you did not discuss it with the other party first."

Meanwhile, he apologized and said, "Whatever you feel, I will respect that." I said thank you. We went on and continued to see each other. After that, I was comfortable to accept his offer and become his girlfriend. We went out a lot and did different things, like double-dated with his parents, went to parties, had family picnics, had family reunion with both sides of the family, went to church, and took family photos. He was so nice and respectful.

I remember my boyfriend. My brother and I went walking down the street. There were some people passing out a flyer saying you can get free testing for AIDS. My boyfriend was rapping about how he was healthy, and he was tested already. As we were approaching the clinic, there were people outside directing us inside the clinic. They were telling us where to go for the testing. This was the clinic that my mother used to always take us for our checkups, as well as the kids in the neighborhood. It was a free clinic for people in our neighborhood that could not afford health insurance. At that time, when we went, they were giving free testing for AIDS. They asked us if we wanted to get tested. We said yes. After we got our blood taken, they asked us to come back in a week or two weeks for the test results. When we came back, they asked us to go upstairs, and they gave us each our results. By the grace of our God, we were fine. My boyfriend said, "I told you I was healthy, but it is good to know for your own safety." When we were leaving, this girl had bad news. She was yelling and crying. I felt so sad for the young lady.

My mom liked him a lot. She said he was so respectful. My oldest son even liked him a lot. He was about three years old. He nicknamed my son Popcorn, and everybody else in his family called him Popcorn. I thought that was so cute—Popcorn.

We eventually got engaged. He proposed at my job. The ring was beautiful because I can be very picky. He moved in with me at my mother's house so he can help get our own place. This was too good to be true. They always say what is in the dark will come out in the light. I remember when I found out that I was pregnant because I was being intimate or sexually active with him, and I started to bleed. Then I had to go to the hospital that night. My boyfriend and my brother took me to the hospital. They stayed with me in the waiting room, and then they left and said they will be right back. The doctors called me in, and they checked me. That was when they told me I was pregnant. I left the hospital looking all around for my boyfriend and my brother. Then I noticed the car, and I started to approach the vehicle. When I approached the vehicle, I paused because I saw my brother and my boyfriend sniffing cocaine up their nose.

They never knew I saw them using drugs. I had no idea that they were users. I was shocked and upset. I said to myself, I wish I knew this before I got pregnant. Then I kept thinking, Why show me this now and not before I was carrying a child. I made noises to let them know I was there so they can stop what they were doing. I got in the car and told them that I was pregnant. They were happy, but I was not at all. I was thinking I did not want to have a baby with someone that uses drugs. I did not say anything. I kept it to myself.

We were still planning to get married. We went to counseling at the church several times. I noticed how things were changing. He started hanging out with my brother a lot and not paying me any attention. I would come from work and go to my room, and he would always be in the room with my brother. My father would come over and say things to my mother, "Why are two men in the room with the door closed all the time? That is not healthy at all." My father would also say, "He needs to be paying my daughter some attention especially because she is pregnant. Why is he fixing breakfast for him and my son? He did not even ask if my daughter wanted to eat." I felt so invisible in this relationship. There was so much going on especially because I was pregnant. I felt trapped in another relationship that was going sour. This was not looking good for me at all again.

My father always came over and made a fuss. "That's not healthy, Louise. I don't care what problems you may have or what you try to hold on to by keeping it covered up. It's always going to leak out. No matter how many skeletons you have hidden. God will truly reveal it."

Remember, every relationship is designed to perform with kindness, gentleness, respectful, and loving at the beginning, but down the road, it also leads to or hold a different task or agenda that holds issues or problems behind the mask of lies. If they're not being real or truthful to mankind, it will hold by leading into destructions. The mask of lies.

I remember my boyfriend's mother called me and said, "Steve told me to call you and let you know he did not want to get married." I said, "What do you mean? We planned this. We're done sending out invitations and everything." She said, "If he does not want to get married, you cannot make him. He's not ready." His mother said, "I am sorry, but that is not what he wants—to get married." Then she hung up. I was through with this. I started getting upset, and I did not know what to do at all. I literally had to go to everyone, especially my coworker, to let them know what happened and that there was not going to be any wedding. This was so embarrassing. When I look back on this, God's plans were a beautiful master plan. This was only for my good, but I didn't know at that time. I did not say nothing to him. I just kept focusing on myself and the baby. My boyfriend was not around that much. He would come home from work sometimes and go into the room or stay out. He had a good job working at the hospital. Then when he started getting deep into himself and not showing up for work, he got fired.

One night, I was in the room asleep, and my father came and woke me up and said, "You need to come down the street to get Steve. Your brother and Steve are fighting down the street." I asked, "Why are they fighting?" My father said, "I do not know. Just come on." My father drove me down two blocks. It was terrible. I've never seen my brother so upset like this before. They were all in the street throwing words back and forth. My brother was throwing punches, and Steve was bleeding from the face. There was not anything I could do because I was pregnant. One thing I know is that it had to be something serious for my brother to be so upset, and it is hard to calm him down. I still did not know, after everything was over, what happened. Everyone was not saying anything. I was still in the dark about everything.

However, I went to a hotel with my boyfriend so he can cool off. I came back home, and he went on to his family house. I never knew and let it pass. I remember while I was staying with my mother, she gave me a newspaper and told me to fill out an application that was pertaining to Section 8. She said, "Fill it out. You never know what can happen, and I will mail it out." However, months later, some papers had come from the Section 8 Housing Authority telling me to come into their office. I told my mother about it and said to her, "What do you think? They want me to fill out more paperwork?" She said, "I do not know. You have to find out when you go to your appointment." I went to my appointment, and they asked me to sit down in the waiting area. As I was waiting, I noticed how a lot of people were coming into the waiting area. I did not think anything of it at first until they asked everybody that was there to follow them into the back. So another lady and I looked at each other, puzzled. Soon as we got into the backroom, this lady from the office said, "I know everyone wants to know what is going, so I am here to announce that you all officially have Section 8." Everyone was screaming with joy, smiling, and laughing. The lady from the office made another statement and said, "Congratulation to everyone. Just know you were the pick that was chosen."

She also said, "Just know there are going to be some jealous people who are going to be mad." Then she gave us our voucher that had the number of bedrooms that was according to our family sizes. She told us we had three months to find something or we can lose it. I was so happy. I could not believe this was happening to me. This was right on time. If it was not for my mother telling me to fill out this application that the Section 8 Housing Authority placed in the newspaper, this would never had happened for me at all. This was truly a blessing.

Soon as I got my paper, I immediately started looking for an apartment with the help of my brother-in-law and sister. We found a place in Irvington, New Jersey. My first apartment. I was excited but nervous as well because I was so used to being with my mother. I was a mother with a child and pregnant with another one on the way, but my mother taught me well as a young lady. The landlord was nice. She knew this was my first apartment. She let me come in without having the whole security. She said I can give it to her when I can and she would work with me. My brother-in-law helped me move into the apartment. Soon after that, my boyfriend came and moved in with me. I felt a little safe because I was pregnant and had my oldest son.

That was the biggest mistake: I allowed him to live with me. Things were going well. He cooked, he washed clothes, and we had cookout in the backyard. Do not get me wrong, he is a good-hearted man, but he was a man that carry secrets (skeletons in his closets) in his life. He was still battling drugs, among other issues. I remember the light bill came, and we were discussing over the bill. So being that he was not working, I gave him money to get a money order for the light bill. He takes the money and did not show up for a couple of days. When he did show up, I asked him about the money order, and he said he spent the money (drugs). I was heated up. I told him you better give me back my money, and I do not care how you get it back. I argued him down like nothing was to it. There were so many signs in front of me, but I did not face reality nor take heed to it for what it was. My eyes were covered because my heart and feelings were getting the best of me again.

I can remember he took money again that was for laundry. I came home and saw a tub full of clothes he was washing because he spent the money. My son's father tried to make up for what he had done. This was his way of making sure the clothes were clean after the fact he spent the laundry money. We would go spend time at his parents' house. Steve would leave me and the baby at the parent's house. I would call him on the phone to see when he was coming back to pick us up. He would say he was on his way. Then he never showed up, and his parents would be upset. Then his parents would take me and the baby home. He would always be in and out the house, and he did not come back for days, or he would call and say he's taking care of some business. There was one time he did not even come back home for weeks. He called me one night and said he was detoxing, and he did not want to come around me. I said, "You trying to detox on your own really and not getting help through a program?" This most definitely did not work for him at all.

He would have strange guys come to the house, and I would question him a lot. I would ask him why his friends dress like that, talk feminine, or walk a certain way. He would get mad and be very defensive. He would say that was none of my business. He said I should not question things about his friends and stop judging.

He would stay on the phone talking to this one guy for hours all the time. He even had the guy come over to the house, and they would be in the living room all night. Then I would question him about it again, and he would say they're friends and he's going through some things right now. It just did not seem normal to me, especially if you are sitting on the couch close on each other and always talking secretly. There was a lot of things going on that disturbed me, especially when he stated that the landlord's boyfriend was trying to come on to me. Which I thought it was ridiculous because I only met the man one time since I had been living in the apartment for about three years. My landlord and her boyfriend were respectable people. God gave me favor through the landlord by moving in with no security.

My brother-in-law and my son's father used to work together at a moving company. My son's father Steve and brother-in-law worked at Sears shampooing carpets together. My brother-in-law used to always try and tell me about my son's father about things he thought was weird or unhealthy for a man. One day, my brother-in-law came over to the house to talk to me because he was disturbed about something. He said, "Sister-in-law, I do not want to see you get hurt by nobody, and it is my job to be there for you and my nephews." He never really said what was on his mind. He just said be careful and watch out for yourself.

My brother-in-law was not married to my sister at the time of this event that took place in my life. My brother-in-law said a guy approached him as he was approaching my house one day. My brother-in-law said the guy seen him coming to my house and approached him. They knew each other by his grandmother babysitting my sister and brother-in-law's kids and my baby boy. The guy said, "I wanted to talk to Cathy about me and Steve being together." He said he was catching feelings for Steve and was falling in love with him. He was letting my brother-in-law know that him and Steven were sleeping together. The guy was coming to talk to me about my son's father, but instead he vented out to my brother-in-law (Elizabeth Avenue, Irvington, New Jersey). My brother-in-law and Steven fought at the job and got fired after he addressed him about the situation among other things. My brother-in-law said he was not going to hurt my sister-in-law.

I never knew about this guy until now, when I asked my brother-in-law what was it at that time when he wanted to talk to me about until this day (November 2019). My brother-in-law never told me about this event that took place. They always had words because my brother-in-law knew about his identity. I never in my life could imagine a man can be with a man. An to be honest, they look like regular guys because I always seen actual gay guys who does dress, look, walk, and talk in a feminine way that you knew head-on who they represent in the gay club. Nowadays, they look and act like regular guys who are dating females and married to them as well. This is what throws you off your guard (the unrevealing shadow walker). During those times, you did not think nothing of it because it was not so open to the public in a serious matter until AIDS broke out. That is when it became serious about gay men and contracting the virus. I was young and did not know so much about men with men. It was not so serious back in the olden days. If you are not familiar or aware of these things, it would not click in your mind until something takes place that catches your attention.

I remember I was home that night, and I got a phone call from Steve's sister. She was trying to forewarn me about sleeping with her brother because he's not doing right. She also said, "Did my mother call you because we were talking about my brother and concerned about you and the kid's safety. I do not want you to get hurt or for something to happen to you, so please stop sleeping with him." Family holds secrets as well to protect their own.

I believed in my heart she was warning me, but she never said what he was doing. I did not say too much on the phone with his sister because I was just being a listener. I was amazed because she called me that night, and soon after the call that next week, I got another phone call. This phone call was shocking because the night I received the call, I was lying in my bed. I answered, and a man spoke in a feminine voice. The voice and said, "Is this Cathy?" I said yes. Then the guy said, "I have Steve right here, but he's scared to talk to you about his problem. I told him he needs to be open with you about us." Then I heard another voice that said, "No, don't do that." The guy said, "Well, she needs to know." And then the phone clicked off. I never heard anything else after that phone call. I was shocked. I could not believe what I heard that night. On that note, I did not address it to Steve at all. I kept it to myself. I did not even sleep with him as well just from the two phone calls I received.

We always got into fights and arguments a lot. It was one argument when he tried to take my baby boy. He said, "I am taking my son, and I am going to my mother's house to live." One thing about me is that I do not play around with nobody when it comes to my kids. My kids are my life, and I will protect them by any means necessary. When he said that, something inside me struck a nerve. I said, "Oh no! You are not taking my baby out of here." At that time, I was holding my baby, and he reached out and grabbed him. We were playing tug of war because he was not leaving the house with my baby. He had my baby's legs, trying to pull him from me.

We were all over the kitchen. Things were breaking, such as the chairs, and table broke down. I was determined that he was not getting my child. I told my mother, and she informed me to call my father. I called my father and told him my son's father was trying to take my baby. My father was so upset. He said, "Tell that nigger to get out your house, and he better be gone before I get there." My father kept yelling and threating him the whole time on the phone. Steve did not listen to my father at all. He kept on coming after the baby. My father showed up, and he was angry. He told Steve, "You need to leave now before I throw you out." I was always puzzled of how my father got to my house that fast. My father lectured me for hours about the situation. He said, "You do not need nobody like that at all, who is going to mistreat you and your kids. Let him go by his own business."

When my father came to my rescue, I was so happy he was there for me. He did not have to worry about my son's father coming back as of that day. I went on with my life. I did not hear from Steve in a couple of months until I got a phone call from him. He stated that he was going away to work at this job with his brother. It was a magazine company where they would travel around the world and sell magazines from door to door. He wanted me and the baby to come over to his parents' house because they were giving him a going-away dinner. We came over that night, and my baby walked for the first time. I was so excited to see my baby walk. His father left that next day to go on his journey.

Doing his journey in traveling for months, he never called and asked how his son was doing. He'd only been to two of his birthday parties since he was born, and he hardly even sent money to help out with his son's finances. However, the only time I got money was when he got arrested twice for child support and he could not be released until he paid the balance off on the back-child support. Also, when his mother spoke to him, he sent money through Western Union.

There was one time when his sister called me and said Steve paid her light bill and gave her money for food. Then he turned around and sent more money to his mother taking care of her needs. I was so upset with this and decided to talk to him about it. My son's father called me one day and said, "My mother said you were trying to reach me." His family was the only one that had his contact number. I said yes, and he asked me if I was seeing someone. I told him yes (he got very quiet for a moment), and he asked about his son. I then asked him why he was giving money to take care of his family's needs and not his own flesh and blood.

He aggressively said he can do whatever he wanted to do because that is his mother and family. I said, "What do you mean? Your son comes before your family's needs. If anything, you should be taking care of your son's needs and not everybody else's needs. Your son is your priority." He in turn said, "You need to get your man to take care of what you want for your son." I said, "That is not his responsibility. My son has a supposed to be father that needs to handle his responsibilities as a father." We kept on going back and forth until my mother picked up the other phone and said, "Catherine, I raised you better than that. You do not need to beg any man to take care of their responsibilities at all. If my grandson has you and his grandparents, he will be all right." My mother said, "As of today, give it to God. Let God handle it and let it go now. It is not worth your time. Get off this phone now."

I was quiet. I did not respond after my mother had spoken. I just hung up the phone, and I never looked back. Years later, my son's father reached out to me and said he was in town. He asked if he could see his son, and I said yes. We hang out, and he spent time with his son. My son's father asked if he can come over to my house and stay the night. I did not mind at all because we were on good terms with each other, and that was a good thing in my book. He came over, and we ate out, laughed, and talked. During this time, my mother was living with me, and she left to go down south to visit family. Meanwhile, my son's father and I went upstairs to chill, and he tried to come on to me. But I was not feeling him like that anymore (my feelings were completely gone from him). I brushed him off to let him know there was nothing going down between the two of us at all. My heart was with someone else at that time, and I knew about his lifestyle. He left the next day, and I did not hear from him since then.

My mother had called me and said she was trying to reach me for the longest time. I told her I never heard the phone ring, and I was in and out of the house. She said Prophetess Jackson was trying to reach me, and it was important. My mother said, "I am going to have her call you now when I hang up from you." Prophetess Jackson called me and said I was in her spirit, and she needed to talk to me. She said, "God told me to tell you that there was a man who was coming to hurt me and he knows he's sick. He wants to destroy your life. You should not have sex with him. Be very careful." I came to learn that my son's father had contracted the virus AIDS from having sex with men (a double secretive life). I remember when the family had to fly him back to New Jersey because he got sick at his job. Once he arrived, they immediately rushed him to the hospital. The family and I would pay him a visit from time to time. I asked my son if he wanted to see his father and that it was his choice. I also said that your father is very sick, and he might not make it. My youngest son was about eight years old at that time, and he decided he wanted to see him. His father talked to him, and he apologized for not being in his life. I remember when I was alone with him in the room, and he told me everything about his double life. He told me that he was seeing this guy for a while, but he noticed how he would take these certain pills every day, and by him being a nurse aide working in the hospital, he kind of got a feeling about the pills. He knew something was not right. He eventually approached him about it, and the guy got very upset and broke their relationship. (The guy he was dating was sick with the virus). He also told me the guy had a girlfriend at that time as well while seeing him. I told him I always knew about his lifestyle, but that was his life if he wanted to be with men. It was his choice. He also told me how he found out he contracted the virus AIDS. He said he was out working going from door to door selling magazines when a big bug bites him on his arm. He did not think anything of it because he was nourishing or nursing it. However, when he did notice that it was not getting any better, it got worse. The wound was not healing properly, so he went to the hospital, and they tested him. This was how he found out he was sick. He stays in his hotel room all that time and grew sicker and sicker until his nephew at that time was working there as well had to notify the family of his condition. The family paid for an air flight due to his condition. He also asked me not to inform the court that he was up here because he does not want to go to jail sick like this. I told him I would not do anything like that to him. I kept my word because I am not a cruel person.

I was too blind to see it at that time. My chapter from him closed when he told me on his bed of affliction he was sorry he hurt me. He wished he could take it all back and make it right. He also said, "I cannot believe you're standing by my side despite all the pain I brought you through and not being there for my son. How could you still be here for me after I treated you wrong?" I responded by saying my mother always taught me that when people treat you wrong, you still show love and kindness as God shows us. I also said, "My mother raised me better than that. I am not going to turn my back on people and you are my son's father." He just cried and said he was truly sorry, and he wished he could be the man that he should have been in my life.

When I was there in the hospital, I helped feed him and gave him something to drink. I would visit him occasionally from time to time. I remember one day, I could not make it, and his sister called me from the hospital and said Steve was upset. She said he wanted to know why I did not come and did he do something to upset me. I said, "No, tell him I had an appointment to go to that is why I could not make it to visit him. I would be there tomorrow. Do not worry yourself."

My son's father passed away on July 17, 2005. It was hard to see him go, but with the love and support of the family and friends, the funeral was pleasant and loving.

Chapter 7

THE POWER OF FORGIVENESS

My mother always said that when people mistreat you or do you wrong, God has their number. She also said they must come back and repent of their wrongdoing before they leave this world. She said they must make it right, whether they were on their bed of affliction or not. She told me I should not worry about it because it's in God's hands. She also said, "You do not do evil or mistreat people for doing you wrong because you will also be put in the same category as them. You pray for them by giving them to God and letting him handle your hurt and pain. You still show love, and you do not have to be in their company but treat them with a long hand of spoon and keep it going in your life."

It was not my job to show hurt toward anybody that have mistreated me because my life was being counted for the things I do. I am a person who still has a good heart with lots of compassion. I did not allow the hurt and pain again turn me into a sour or a vicious person. I do not have to do the things that people do that is wrong in this world but do better as God wants me to be in his glory. I asked God to forgive me for mistreating or hurting anyone in this world. I want to make it to heaven. The Bible say repent every day even if you sin or not (Luke 17:4).

I have moved on from all those old badges.

The reason why my brother and Steven had a big fight is because, my mother said, Steven tried to come on to him while they were in the room together.

My brother said while he was sitting in the chair, Steve was giving him a haircut, and he noticed how he was stroking his hands across his hair in a feminine way. He said only females stroke his hair like that with their hands, not a males. My brother did not feel right how Steve was doing his head, like stroking it. My brother jumped out of the seat and said, "Man, what you are doing?" They started arguing and fighting in the house to a point where it escalated outside. This is where my brother came across with words and started to fight. My brother may get high, but he had sense enough to know when something was wrong. My brother is straight up a ladies' man. My mother said, "Your brother said he used to hear rumors about Steve when they were locked up together." He didn't think nothing of it, but when he thought back, he knew it was true about him and other guys' performance.

My mother said he told Steve, "Man, you go with my sister, and you knew you was like that. You are not going to marry her straight up. If you knew you had a problem with liking guys, you should have been straight up with my sister." My brother warned Steve that he better let me know or he was going to come after him. He said, "You are not going to hurt my sister." My mother said Steve came to her and said, "Can I talk to you?" They took a drive and talked at Westside Park. This was where he opened up and told my mother everything about his sexuality. My mother said Steve was well-mannered, but he had a problem. He never disrespected her, and he always gave her respect. Steve never came to me personally and opened up to me at all about his sexuality. I never knew about the secret he told my mother until he was out of my life. I became very upset at the fact that she told me only now. This could have been dealt with, and I would have never perceived on with this man. My mother said, "I did not want you to think I was breaking up your relationship." I had to learn in my own way in putting pieces together, especially from the strange phone calls I was receiving warning me about this man. God protected me even when his family never disclosed this information. I was kept in the dark. I proceeded in a relationship with this man even though my own family kept me in the dark by giving that person the responsibility to unfold their own darkness to me, the one who knew nothing. It was because they felt like they did not want to seem like they were trying to break up a relationship. Oh really? I am not that type of person to not want to be told the truth, especially if it came from my own family member. I truly do not indulge myself in that type of relationship. If that is how you want to live your own life being with men, then so be it. That is your life, not mine. I am not the one to judge your lifestyle, only God. I would love you and give you something if you are in need, but I will not take a part in that type of behavior. The Bible says it all, and I truly stand by that. Steve told me one day how his second oldest sister and youngest brother's father hit him with a blackjack across his head, and when he came to, he was on top of him, having sex with him. He said he was about eight or nine years of age when this situation took place in his life. He also said his mother took him and washed him up in the tub due to the bleeding and held him on her bed. She never took any action of the sexual assault that was performed on her son. She never sought help for her child. Steve conserved his problem all the way up into his adult life without any help in facing his dilemmas.

He felt like that was normal to be with men due to his sexual abuse as a child.

Steve was in love with my brother. His statement was nobody understands him the way Raheem (James) does. He took my brother's kindness the wrong way, and he didn't find out until the hard way. My brother had a good heart, and he can be good friends with anybody. Just don't double-cross him or do something that makes him feel uncomfortable because he will come out of his shell hard at you. My brother did visit Steve in the hospital, and he told my brother what happened. My brother asked him why he laid around all that time in his hotel room sick and did not say nothing. He said that he was embarrassed and ashamed of himself. My brother also asked, "Why didn't you use protection if you were having sex with men?" He just held his head down and felt too hurt and ashamed. My brother never returned to visit him because he says he could not see him that way. I realize now why Steve called off the wedding due to my protective brother and mother. Rest in peace, my big brother (JCH Jr.) in heaven. Love you and miss you always.

My son's father gave his life to the Lord while on his bed of affliction. If God can forgive him in spite of, why can't we in spite of our own circumstances forgive others as well? God can give you that agape love that goes beyond or higher in any means of your life. An agape love that is an unconditional love that bears all things through how the world may come at you in all angles in a sinful way. This is a message that will lead to a healing process of your soul.

Fourth Relationship and Last

I was seeing another guy later after Steve and I was over. I can remember when this guy named Kevin came into my life. He was eight years younger than me. I met him through my best friend Lakeisha's fiancé. This happened through a phone conversation, which I was having with my best friend. She told me that her fiancé came over to her house with his friend. His friend wanted to say hi to me, which I did not mind. After that, I had a phone call. It was Kevin, and I said, "How did you get my number?" He said, "Your girlfriend gave me your number." I told him she would not do that unless she asked me first. Eventually, he was honest and told me the truth that he told her I said he can have my number. I let him know that it was wrong and he already started lying to me and that was not good at all. He said he was sorry. He just wanted my number because he liked my voice. I told him you need to apologize to my best friend as well.

However, time went on, and I can remember the first time he came to my house. He called me and asked me if he can see me. I agreed because I wanted to meet him as well. This was the first time we met each other. When he came to my apartment in Irvington, New Jersey, I went downstairs to open the door. I did not open it right away. I looked through my peephole to see what type of guy he was. He had a big polar bear coat on, and I looked around him. I did not see a car at all. I opened the door, and we said hi. He wanted to come upstairs to my house, but I hesitated and said my kids were in the bed and I do not know if this good time. He said his ride had left and was coming back later to pick him up. I said okay, and we went into my house. He went to my living room to sit down. My girlfriend called me to ask if he arrived at my house. I said yes. As I was on the phone with her, I investigated my living room and noticed him sitting down and taking off his boots. I told my best friend I couldn't not believe this dude was taking his boots off in my house like he knew he belonged there. I told her, "If you are going to take your shoes off, make sure your socks are right." He had a hole in his socks and had the nerve to cross his legs. We laughed so hard about it. I never seen this happen to me before. This man was truly bold.

    I eventually hung up with her, and I went into my living room. We started to chat a little bit. He asked to use the bathroom, and I showed him. As I turned, he tried to come on to me. Wow! Men sure do not hesitate at all. I told him I am not that kind of person. He left. I knew he walked wherever he was going. I remember my mom and dad came over to my house, and they had bought a couple of pizzas, fried chicken, and soft drinks. My friend Kevin was over, and I introduced him to my family. My mother and I were fixing plates for the kids and my dad. My mother told me to ask my friend if he wanted to eat as well, and he said yes. My mother then said, "Boy, he sure did not hesitate. He answered quickly." We prayed over the food and ate. This was nice.

    Kevin kept coming over, and we started going out to dinner, movies, family, and friends' gathering. One day, he came over early, and I had just come in from shopping for my kids. I decided to pick him up a couple of items such as socks, T-shirts, and underwear. I felt bad when I saw how his socks were when I met him that day. He was so surprised to see what I brought him stuff. He said he never had girls buying him things because he would be the one always taking care of the females. He said, "Thank you very much." I learned he did not have a job, and he was living with his sister and cousins. He had just come home from a program he was in.

    I remember talking to Kevin on the phone about sex. I told him I was not going to lay down with no other man unless they take an AIDS test for my safety and my kids'. I told him I have just seen how my best friend Darnette and my youngest son's father went through with that disease. I was more cautious with my life. He said that it is good because he had just taken the test and he will bring it to me to show his results. He was negative from the disease. It was legit.

    I still had him wait until I was ready. He said I was the only girl that ever put him through this before and that I was different from the rest of them. I said yes, I was just not that type to rush anything now. He was still trying to anyway after a few months. I eventually gave in, but I was nervous. He handled it very well. However, as time went on, they held another problem just as you would think everything was going well. Sometimes, in your trials and tribulations, you never know what situation you may face in this lifetime.

I did everything in this relationship with Kevin. He did not have to worry about anything. I had the apartment, a good job, my own car, a nice bank account, and was attending college. Life was feeling good to me as a mother, having a man, and being a church girl. He had nice clothes, a sharp haircut, and money in his pocket. I always have a good heart when it came to doing things and supporting people. I loved spending money shopping for my kids, myself, and sometimes others.

In this relationship, as time went by, months and years later, I came to realize and see how this relationship was. Kevin had his own personal agenda of good deeds of doing things by me in reference to going place with me at my expense such as out to dinner, movies, family functioning, or events and parties that was given by my job, driving me around, giving me gifts, cleaning the house, cooking dinner, and supporting me in school.

Kevin's only attention at that time was being there for things that I can offer at his own lack of needs. This person's bad side was a man who hurt me and caused me lots of pain. He took advantage of my heart and love just to benefit his own needs. I remember when I went food shopping with my girlfriend for my children. I came home, and he helped me with the groceries by putting them away.

We started to take out all the food from the grocery bag, which was all over the floor, stove, and table. He started to ask angrily why I bought pork because he did not eat pork. I said, "Oh, I forgot you did not eat pork, but there are other food besides pork I bought." My best friend Lakiesha was sitting at the table and watching everything. Kevin started yelling and saying I was trying to be funny, that I knew he did not eat pork. Then he started to kick the grocery around and stomp on it. I got in a rage and said, "I bought this food, and you do not kick or stomp on food I brought, especially for my kids. This is not right! You are wrong, and you need to get out of my house." I felt like whether I brought pork or not, what gave him the right to say anything unless his money helped providing groceries. The unrevealing shadow walker is slowly showing his demeanor (character).

Later, he called and apologized, and I forgave him.

Throughout the relationship, he began to show me what else he had hiding in his life. I used to let him drive my car even if I knew he did not have a license. I thought that was okay because he was my man, and I was tired of driving a lot. He would run errands for me by taking me to work and picking me up, taking me to stores, picking up lunch, and most of the time, he would use the vehicle for his own pleasure. Kevin used to take my car and hang out with his friends at night and came back home the next day. He would drop me off and my kids at my best friend Darnette's house so he can hang with friends. I used to call him several times when I am ready to be picked up, and he would say he's coming and do not show up. Then the kids and I would have to stay overnight because he would abandon us.

This went on for as long as I can remember, along with other problems such as the following:

1. He was cheating on me.

2. He was taking my money out of my pocketbook when I go to sleep at night. I would hide my money in my bra or under my pillow.

3. He called me out by my name.

4. He put his friends before me.

5. He left me in my house with no food to eat for me and my kids because he took my car and did not show up for a couple of days later, I would call him, and he would not answer. Then I would call from the payphone, and he would pick up. He would say he's coming but never showed up for days. I would have to feed my kids with whatever little scrap I had to give them. It did not matter whether I ate or not as long as my kids ate. I cried every day and my kids had to be a witness

to see their mother in that state of mind. Sometimes my son would miss school because of Kevin's actions of not bringing back my car.

6. He was a liar, player, and a conniving and deceitful person.

7. He was selfish and always think about himself.

8. He would stay at the building all the time with his friends late at night until four, five, or eight in the morning. He then would call me to pick him up. We would argue because I had my kids in the bed sleeping, and he would want me to pick him up because he did not have a ride. Then I would eventually give in and leave my kids in the bed to go pick him up.

9. He would take my vehicle and have tickets and bullet holes on it, and my car would end up in the pound Then I would have to take my hard-earned money to get it out.

10. I remember I was blessed with a lumpsum of money, and I got a store with it so that my family can have something and earn money to keep our finances going. However, that did not work out because my boyfriend wanted to sell drugs in the store along with his friends. I was not having it because this was in my name, and I was looking out for my kid's well-being. I took it all back and said no. Then he got upset with me and left. Then my store got robbed, and I confronted my boyfriend because someone had a key to get in, and he was the only one beside me to have a key to the store. They made it seem like somebody came in and robbed the store, but the whole time, my boyfriend had it set up to be robbed.

11. I would see how he looks at my friends (lustful ways) and play around them in a disrespectful way. He never ever jokes or play around me like that ever, and to see your man play around or look at your friends and family in a certain way is very hurtful and disrespectful.

12. He would have condoms in his wallet and telephone numbers of girls. I remember one day I went to court with him, and he reached in his wallet to get something, and I saw a picture of a girl with a child. I questioned him about it, and he said it was a friend. I asked why would he have a picture of a

girl in his wallet anyway when he did not have a picture of me in the first place. I also said, "Do you see a picture of a man in my purse? I am the one supporting and sitting in court with you, not her or your friends." I was silent the whole time we were in court.

I was a faithful, respectful, and supportive girlfriend to Kevin throughout our relationship. He did not have to worry about me at all, but I had to worry about his fidelities. I did so much for him and his family. I paid his probation fines of $35 dollars every week faithfully, and I went with him to pay for it. I took care of his daughter when she was two years old, bought her clothes and toys, did her hair, fed her, loved her like she was my own child, and took her everywhere I went—to a friend's house and church. My family adored her, gave and did for her like she was their grandchild as well. I remember Kevin came to me and asked me if his daughter can stay with us because her mother was going through a crisis. I said yes without hesitating. I immediately enrolled her into day care at my job. My boss understood what was going on, and she took her in. I brought her book bag, blanket, and I paid for her tuition. She was like a daughter I always wanted. Eventually, she went back to her mother when she was suitable to have her back.

Kevin came to me again about his sister and asked me if his sister and her three kids can stay with us because he did not want to see his nieces and nephew out in the street. I thought about it and spoke to my kids to let them know as well. I said yes even though I had a small two-bedroom apartment. She stayed with us for a couple of months until she got back on her feet. His sister helped a lot with food and money. I just had to stay on her about being clean. I am a clean and organized person. I can't stand messiness or filthiness at all. I loved his sister and her kids to death. They are my world. She ended up staying with me twice. I helped support her and the children's needs. They were my family, and I would do it all over if I had to again. My heart goes out to people because of my passion of helping someone in crisis, just being a friend to talk to or listen. I also took in his mother and made sure she was comfortable and taken care of. It was always stated you should never bite the hands that feed you, clothe you, and take care of you. This is so true because people sometimes forget all the things a person have done for them, and they turn around and give you hell. That is an ungrateful soul that does not care about nothing but themselves selfishness (the unrevealing shadow walker).

    I did a lot for Kevin and his family to the point my kids were feeling left out. They felt like their mother was taken away from them, and my oldest son would be rebellious against me because of his hurt inside. My oldest son and youngest son have seen a lot of growing up. They did not care for my boyfriend because they see how he was mistreating me, and they have seen my tears a lot. This was not good at all for my kids to grow up and see. Kevin did not play a good role model as a man in my children's life at all. I knew all this about Kevin, but because of my heart (love), I forced my name on it because of my own wants and needs. I love my soldiers (kids) to death, and I would do anything for them. I did not want to hurt them like that. I just wanted to try to please everyone's needs being a caring person as I am. I did a lot with my kids. I was very protective over them. I stayed with Kevin for a long time as an on-and-off relationship. I remember when I was working at my job and I did not hear from Kevin, so I gave him a call early that day. As I was talking to him, he was kind of not so talkative. Then I heard a girl's voice in the background. I said, "You have company." He said yes. Then I said, "You with this person?" He said yes again, and then I said, "So I guess I won't be calling you no more then." He said yes and goodbye. God does not like ugliness at all. I told my girlfriend what happened, and she was very upset and said that it was his loss. She also said he was going to need you before you need him. I was in a relationship with this man, and he was lying up with another woman and had the nerve to be calm about it, like it was nothing. I eventually moved on and thought nothing of it. I was good. I had everything going for myself including college, a car, apartment, and a job paying pretty good money. It was not like he was taking care of me and my kids. I was taking care of him, and I was good.

    However, weeks or months went by. I was at my job, and someone told me I have a phone call. I went to answer the phone, and behold it was Kevin. He said, "How you been?" I said fine, and he said, "Can I ask you for a favor?" I said, "A favor? Are you serious? You're the one with a girl over your house, and you made up your mind right then and there. You wanted to be with her and kicked me to the side." He said, "I know, and I was wrong, but I was wondering if you can give me a couple of hundred dollars for rent." He was living in an apartment with his older sister and cousins. He said the landlord needed the rent money, and they were trying to get some money together so they will not be convicted. He said, "Can you think about it? I really need your help, but I would be fine if you said no or yes." People always say that and know where your heart is especially when they know you are kindhearted.

He got me again. I gave in and gave him the money, but they still ended up being convicted. Kevin ended up living with me at my apartment.

I remember when my brother passed. This was devastating news—to hear of the death of a loved one. I was hurt and angry all at once. I would lash out on my boyfriend and take it out on him. Then we started to argue at each other off and on. He then turned around and left me in a distressed situation. This was where I needed him the most. I could not handle the loss of my only brother. I carried double hurt on my back from the loss of my brother and my boyfriend leaving me two days before the funeral. I had to go through this hurt by myself, without the man I loved. I cried every night by myself, hoping and wishing someone can embrace and hold me and say, "It's going to be all right. I got you. I am here for you." Kevin left and moved down south with his mother. We were separated for about two to three years. I would call him still, feeling hurt. He would still treat me cold as the hell (Satan) below. We eventually worked it out, and he said he was so sorry I had to go through the loss of my brother alone and he shouldn't have listened to the person who told him to go ahead and leave. I went through a lot with this man, but I still accepted his badges because of the love that I had for him. Time and years went on with us having ups and down. Through this, I never stopped having God in my life. I would pray all the time and cry out because of what I'm going through. I used to feel condemned for having a man live with me because of what was taught to me about the Word of God. The Bible says fornication is a sin and abomination and the bed is befouled before God without marriage. I used to feel bad all the time, and guilt was upon me. I used to tell Kevin I was not having sex with him anymore until I get married. That did not go so well because I would end up falling back into the same situation of being intimate. I would also say that God was not pleased with this living without marriage. However, every time I went church, the preacher or the prophet would talk about fornication and adultery. I would feel so bad, but I kept talking to God and letting him know of my circumstances. I did not want to live like this anymore because I wanted to respect God's word. I gave Kevin an alternative to decide—either we get married or we separate. However, he proposed to me on his knees in the closet where I was hanging up some clothes. I thought that was a little awkward, but he was sincere. We were engaged for a while. We've been together for about fifteen years and married about seven years. This was a big turnaround for me from being a girlfriend to being a wife. My mother married us in our North Brunswick apartment on November 08, 2013. We got into arguing with each other the day my mother was setting up to marry us. I said I am not going through with this, and he said, "Come on, I am sorry, and I want to marry you." That was a crazy moment.

I entered a marriage with one saved and the other was unsaved. I knew about his badge, so I did not walk into the marriage of not knowing about this man totally. I did not ask God or even had a conversation with the man in heaven. I did not consult God if this was all right with him. All I knew was I did not want to live in sin anymore. I just told God I love him, and I wanted to be with him and only him. I was settled and in love with my husband. I forced my name on it because of my wants and needs. I was not even thinking about how the future would be as long as I was married now, and things were looking good to me. My husband was working, giving me money, taking care most of the bills, going to church from time to time, and going to college. He also stopped smoking and was slowing down from drinking beer. I prayed hard for this man and my family as well for a change. I was very proud of him for his complete turnaround. We still would argue from time to time, which is normal especially because you are still learning from one another. Sometimes you are going to have a disagreement from time to time, but it is good to set things right between both parties (a clean slate). One thing I did like when we go through our disagreements or issues was we learned to make peace by apologizing even if we are wrong or right.

However, my husband was a stay-at-home husband. What

more could a woman asked for. It was like a dream. I was not working, but I still had income coming in from my disability and my kid's child support/social security and youngest son's deceased father (Steven Sr.) until he was eighteen. I was going to college, and I have completed two bachelor degrees and working on my master. However, that dream went into the dark forest. It began to turn into warfare, and I just got what I wanted because my eyes were focused on my own desires and not keeping a good relationship with the Father in heaven. Things began to change people before my closed eyes. I began to see my husband going back little but shortly into the world of sinfulness. He did dedicate his life to God, but he slid back into the world. When one is not fully saved by fulfilling the gospel of God's statutes or limitation in giving up worldly things completely (backslide) or even have a true righteousness spirit, it's hard to build a good foundation into your relationship or marriage. A person's true self-identity does not show up until later or shortly into the beginning of the relationship. The change had come for us as a family, but the enemy came in and began to use my husband's mind. We must be so careful of letting people into our business because jealousy plays a terrible role among us. Sometimes people will see you are doing well, and they dread to have what you want, and jealousy creeps in and cause unbalance to fall upon you. You must be a watchman upon the wall. Which means you must stay before God in prayer, reading your word, and fasting so the enemy or the shadow walker does not creep in and destroy your wealth or something valuable that you possess.

My husband had his ways, but I did not begin to see it fully until later into the marriage. He would not give me money like he used to. I would get half of his school money, half of the income tax, and get allowance of $300, $200, $150 to $50, $30, $25, $10, $ 6, $5, or no dollars at all. He would say I had to pay the bills, and that was all he had left. I knew he was lying most of the time. He did not pay the entire bills by himself. He used to show me his paystubs and bring home the money to talk about what we're going to take care of together. This was at the beginning of his first job. He used to make sure I had money in my pocket when I had to go out and take care of things.

However, our marriage was not doing so well at all. I was going through this so bad. My husband has been working two jobs, which was a blessing in all. He did not even want to get a second job at all because he would complain. I would encourage him by saying it is going to be fine and the extra income is going to help a lot for us. He would always talk about what he is going to do since he got a second job now. For example, he would say now that he got this second job, he can be able to take me out and spend time with me. We were able to have date nights. He said, "I can give you money because I calculate all the bills, and I would have seven hundred dollars left over. I can give you a couple of hundred dollars and still put up some to save." He also said he would give me until August and I would be able to start doing things. I waited so patiently like I always do to see him fulfill what he had promised to do. It was a lot of promise made, but I've yet to see those promises.

My husband started getting paid and did not offer me nothing. I would go to him and ask for money, and he would say, "I do not have any money. I have to pay the rent, car note, or light bill." I would watch how he lies to me especially at the grocery store. He would say, "I only have $50 or $60 left so we only can get a few things." Then he would say, "What you want then?" I said, "Buy me a case of snapper." Then he says, "What? Do you know how much that cost?" I would say, "You asked me what I wanted." Then I would say never mind, and we went on getting other items. I watched how he was grabbing things and putting it in the cart. When you are not honest or even telling the truth, it shows and tells all the time. We went up to the cash register to buy the grocery, and it came up to $95. He says, "Oh man, I went over into the bill money because you kept putting things into the cart." I said, "Correction. No, you were putting things into the cart. I was just looking because you said you only had $50 or $60." I would feel hurt and mad all at the same time. This was a Friday because we went home and put away all the groceries, and he helped me with my homework. Then he said, "I would be back. I am going to the liquor store." I waited until he came back, but he did not because he called me about going down to Newark to hang out with his friends. I said, "I thought you did not have any money but the bill money?" He said, "My friends are going to treat me," and I said, "Oh really?" He said, "Is that okay?" I said, "I do not agree with this at all." I told my husband I had a problem with it because he was always gone every Friday, leaving me home and do not come back until seven in the morning, drunk. I said, "This is very wrong. It is not right for a married man to leave his home from 6:00 or 7:00 p.m. and do not return until 7:00 a.m. the next day."

I told my husband, "You do not even give me time, take me out, or even give me money. I am supposed to come first before anybody. You've been talking about doing things with me for the longest time, and you rather put your friends before me." He said, "I have not been around my friends for the longest time, and if I want to spend time with them, I can do that. They're going to be my friends, whether you are here are not. You had my time for years, so I am going to give my friends some of my time, whether you like it or not." I said, "So my time is limited because we've been together all these years already. We are married! Why should I have a certain time limit." He said, "I do not want to be in the house like this, bored and working all the time and not having any time for myself. Friday is the only time I can do something."

I said, "What about me? You just going to forget about me. He said, "Go out with your friends." I said, "I do not be with my friends like that. They have their own lives now. If I do go out, I know how to come in a deceit time and my friends knows my status. We have respect for each other's status."

However, men always say the crazy things or do crazy things to benefit their own needs. My husband curses me out and said I was always thinking about myself. The most hurtful thing that my husband has done to me in my life.

The saddest thing about all this was my God would tell me that my husband was not being honest or truthful. God would tell me to just keep praying, do not argue, or get back at him. God would say he will take care of it because I belong to him. God would say, "Hold on, daughter, I got you. I know your hurt and pain."

God also said to me things are going to get worse before it gets better. My God was right because things began to turn for the worse. I never in my life would have expected this to ever happen to me. My husband called me one day that night from working at Amazon (second job). He said, "I have something to tell you. It is not good, and you are going to be mad." He said, "I messed up, babe, bad." I said, "What is it? Are you sick?" He said,

"What, no. There is nothing wrong with me." I said, "Is someone else involved?" He said, "No, babe, but it is bad. I cannot really say it right now because there are people here standing around me. We are really in trouble, and it is my fault." I said, "Just tell me now. Just go ahead and say it." He said, "I'll tell you when I get home. Are you still going to be up when I get there?" I said, "Yes, I will be up, or you can wake me up as well to talk."

My husband came home that morning and lay down, and he never said anything at all. However, I started thinking what it could be because I was worried about the statement he made to me. I said to myself, "Let me check the bills and see if everything was paid." I went and took the bill statements to make a call to check the status. I went downstairs to the living room and made a call to the renter's office, and they told me that I was behind in two months, and the only payment that was put on was $200. I went outside to my car to get the number to call the car dealership. I asked the representor to give me the status update on the payments. The representor stated that I was behind in three months (July, August, and September of 2017) and I need to make a payment to come up depart from not going on my credit report. I was so shocked and furious of what had happened. I called my mother on the phone while I was still in the car, and I started crying badly. My mother then said to me, "What you are saying? I do not understand what you are trying to tell me. Calm down, Catherine, and tell me what happened." I told her, "I do not believe it. All this time I thought he was paying the bills, and he was not at all." My mother said, "What? I told you to go behind him to check for yourself because he was not trustworthy at all." I said, "But I asked him all the time, 'Did you pay the rent, car note, or light bill?' and he told me yes. I do not believe he was lying to me all that time. What I am going to do? We are behind on everything. I cannot believe this is happening right now. He just lied to me." I told my mother I would call her back. I went back into the house and confronted my husband. He was lying in the bed, and I spoke out in anger. I said, "Kevin, why were the bills not paid? Why are we behind in bills? There is no reason we should be behind at all. I asked you if the bills paid and you said yes, it was taken care of." I remember saying to him when he had a phone call from a car dealership. I told him, "If you are going to get a car, let me know so that I can prepare myself." He said, "No, they're always calling me. I am not getting a car." I said, "Whatever, just let me know what is going on. I am perfectly aware of car dealership calling you, and the only way a car dealership will call you is if you give them your information or state that you are interested in a car. That is the only way that they will reach out to you. They do not randomly call you just like that. They do not know anything about you."

People sometimes try to throw a monkey wrench at you to throw you off, but if you listen to them very carefully, you can clearly hear that what they're trying to do is lie. It is what they say that does not make sense to you, and it is even in their body language that shows them up. However, I angrily went off on my husband. He gradually got up and out the bed and went into the bathroom. I was still going off at the mouth, and then he told me, "You always think you are so perfect, and you are never wrong about anything." I said, "This is not about me so do not switch it on me about what you did. You are wrong and how could you look at me every day and have intercourse with me and lie to my face. You knew all the while about this situation, and you kept telling me you took care of it. You said everything is paid, and we are good. You really trying to hurt me, and you do not even care at all." He said, "You act like you never made a mistake. You are so perfect in everything that you do."

I said, "A mistake is, for instance, like getting the wrong direction by failing to understand something correctly, misread the map wrongly and getting lost, or miscalculation you made in counting money. You misunderstood someone's feelings or a mistake in giving someone peanut butter and forgetting that they are allergic to it. A mistake is something you did not tend to do, a judgement that is misguided or wrong. Mistakes are accidents. You know it is wrong, but the wrong word slips out. A mistake is not something that is carried on for a while and have a person believing that it is true, which is a lie. That is something a person attended to do without any conscience of correcting that mistake. Also, it does not fall into category of an error of not knowing or lack of knowledge. You were perfectly aware of your own actions. However, to my understanding, it is not something that is going on for a couple of months that's going to jeopardize us in losing everything."

My husband was asked on several occasions about the bills, and he had the opportunity to correct what was needed to be fixed. My husband is up to something for no good. He's been working, all the while and not paying the bills at all. Where was his money going to because, to my knowledge, it was a setup to corruption, which means that that person had their own hidden agenda.

I was crying hard. Then I ran downstairs and sat in the chair. Then a few minutes later, my husband was coming downstairs. That's when God quickened my spirit and said he was going to make up something. My husband said, "I am going to tell you what happened. I should have told you what was going on." I was still getting on him and said that was no excuse. He said, "Would you listen? You never listen. I need to tell you what happened." He told me, "I saw my friends gambling, and I thought since you always complain about money and talking about your car all the time I figured I would take my paychecks and gamble with the money. I thought that God would bless me in winning a lot of money so I can help both of us out." I said, "God does not bless you in mess. He is against sin, and gambling is one of them. How you figure that God would help by blessing you in that way. He's not a God that would indulge in things like that." He said, "I know, but it was not going to be hurtful to ask and hope anyway. I was feeling good, and I am not going to lie, I felt good about doing it. Everything was going well for a while, and then I was losing."

He said when he loses the money he had put to the side to gamble with and he decided he used the other money for what he had for the bills to gamble with. My husband said he lost everything, and he tried to leave without being noticed. He said he started walking to the car, and they followed him and stop him and asked him where he was going. Then he said they had guns and were trying to take the car, and he told them that it was a renter. Then they took his wallet and started saying out loud his address. He said, "They were repeating the address over and over to the head boss." My husband said he owed them three thousand dollars. He told them that he has a job working at Amazon, and he gets paid every two weeks a thousand dollars. He also told them they can take his credit card where the money was going on, so he can pay them off in six weeks. He said they agree with him, and they told him that they have his address. My husband says he was dealing with the Bloods (gang member). He also stated to my son that he was trying to take the money and buy drugs, but instead, he gambles with it (money). Then he puts up half the money and started winning. Then his friend said, "You might as well go all in." Then he loses everything and tried to walk away. Then the guys approached him with guns. His friend said, "Just pay them off."

I said, "You've got to be kidding me? Are you serious? You put this family in jeopardy like this. I cannot believe this is happening right now. You are so blessed that they did not kill you. You are blessed that prayer was over your life." My husband said they were not going to do anything else. They knew they were getting their money. I said, "What do you mean? These types of people don't care about you or anybody else. If they wanted what was due to them, they going to get it one way or another. They are not saved nor have Christ in their life. These gang people have our address! They can say, 'Forget it, let's go after them.' They can bring harm to me and my son."

My husband started getting smart. He said, "Well, if you were not talking about my car all the time and complaining about going out on Fridays along with everything else, we would never be in this situation." He started cursing and saying, "This is your entire fault. You always want everything your way. You do not care about nobody but yourself." I said, "The blood of Jesus, devil is a liar. This is not about me. This is your own doing, and you started this whole thing because you were not honest at all. You need to take responsibility for your own actions and acknowledge the things that you have done. This is not about nobody else, but you so point the finger at your own self." I started to cry even the more. I said, "You are so wrong of what you have done." Then I started to leave, and he said, "Oh, you're just going to leave like that with everything going on." I said, "You figure it out! You think you know what's best. I don't care anymore."

I left the house and got in my car and drove down the street. I called my mother and told her what happened about my husband's gambling and everything else he stated to me. I was crying hard. I said, "How can he do this to me? What am I going to do?" My mother said, "You need to leave him right there with his mess and go to your sister's house. You do not need to be there, Catherine. There is no telling what would happen when you're there in that house because of his foolishness. Do you want me to call

Vincent [my brother-in-law] to come over there to get you? I do not believe it. My spirit is not receiving what he said about that gang members. Your husband is lying.:

I then told my mother, "I hear the Lord saying, 'Go back and pray for your husband because he is going to need you like never before.' I said, 'What, God? Go to him and pray for him?'" That was when my husband called me on the phone and said, "Where you at?" I said, "I left because I do not want to be there, and I need time to myself." He said, "I am sorry. I should not accuse you. I should have taken responsibility for my own actions. I really need you, and I cannot do this by myself. Can you please come back so that we can talk about it, and I can get ready to go in to work? How long are you gonna take because I don't want to be late for work because we are going to need all the money we can get." I said, "I don't know because I'm hurting right now, but I will be there in a few minutes." I went home, and my husband began to apologize to me, saying he was sorry for everything and he should not blame me for what he had done. He said, "You were right. I needed to look at my own self and take recognition of my own actions and not to blame anyone for it." He also said that it was his fault because he started all this and he was going to fix it. He said, "Also I need you, and I cannot do this by myself." I began to pray with my husband as God instructed me to.

Then my husband prepared himself to leave for work. He said,

"Okay, I am leaving, and I will be back. I will call you as soon as I get a lunch break." I said, "I am not really feeling this because you are going to be fine, and I am here. I do not know what is going to happen." I said, "Anybody can come and break in while I am home and harm me at any time while you are at work safe. These people can change their minds at any time if they choose to." He said, "They are not going to do nothing because they are getting their money. They are not going to take it that far." I said, "How do you know? You cannot predict what they might do. Besides that they are not saved nor have Christ in their life. The enemy can use them to do anything to come up against this family." My husband then said, "It is going to be okay. I am going to lock up everything and call you to check up on you."

I was so angry and afraid for myself. I was so glad my youngest son was spending the summer with his brother in Charlotte, North Carolina (August 10, 2017 to September 28, 2017). I also was feeling paranoid of feeling scared that someone might come to the house and harm me. I would check to see if everything was locked up in the house (windows, door, and garage) every day and every night. I also would lock myself up in my room and put something up against my door for my safety. I never stopped praying. I would keep my TV on all through the night until the morning when my husband got home from working at Amazon. This was so crazy how my husband had put his family in a situation like this because of his selfish or unthoughtful ways. He would call me almost every night when working at Amazon (Sunday through Thursday shift). During the day, I was fine because I would be out taking care of business, or my husband would only work that one job at BJs (Monday, Wednesday, Friday, Saturday, and Sunday for five, six, or eight hours and more for overtime), or he would have off (Tuesday and Thursday). Sometimes his schedule would change up, and he would work straight in a roll. It was not easy living in a situation being fearful for your life.

    At least that was what my husband said to be true. However, as time went on, I was still hurting inside not knowing what to do because the money that my husband was getting was going straight to the bad people he owes money to, as he said. The first job at BJs was paying the child support, which was coming out of that check, along with the Universal Payment Corporation as well. Then things could not get any worse. They started cutting his hours down to three days at BJs. We had nothing to go on for getting out of these debts that he put us in. My husband suggested going get another loan from One Main Financial, so the bills can be caught up. I wasn't feeling this because we already had a loan from them, which was coming out of my disability check along with other things such as health insurance, gym membership, life insurance, renter insurance, and car insurance on both vehicles. My husband was responsible for the rent, car note, cable, light bill, and food. Sometimes I even help with the food as well from time to time.

    I then decided to go ahead along with it because there was no other alternative known but to go that way. I really did not like this. Since it was my husband's fault we were into this mess, he should be getting us out of this situation himself. This was my attitude about this whole situation. We eventually went through the process of getting another loan. I remember sitting in the car with my husband before we went into the office. He took my hand said, "Let us pray," and I followed behind him. It's amazing how man can know how to pray when they are in a bad situation and they ask God for help when they want him to come on in to help them out of a dilemma. Wow! We wanted to get five thousand, but they only approved us for a thousand. This was because we did borrow money already a year ago. My god we were having a little difficulty, but the grace of God was on our side. I never stop praying and fasting before my God. I would cry out to God every day, saying, "God, please do it for my family. The One Main Corporation needed to take picture of the truck we used as collateral again. This was where the problem came in because the truck was broken down due to needing a whole new engine for the vehicle. We told them that the vehicle was not running properly at this time. When explaining the situation, they said, "We cannot go along in giving you a loan unless we have the vehicle here to check it and take photo for our record." The head supervisor came over and heard about our situation. She said for us to go home and get the other documents and come back. She would talk it over with the manager. My heart began to get a little worried. When we came home and gather up what she needed from us, shortly after, the manager himself gave us a call. He said, "I was told about the situation you have. You are having difficulty with bringing the vehicle to the office." We said, "Yes, the vehicle is here in our driveway, not drivable at this moment until we fix it." The manager said, "Do not worry, I am just going to write it up that the vehicle is safely at your residence and go ahead and approve of the loan." He said, "We are here late so come back so that we can get you all set up so you can receive your loan." I said, "Thank you, God, for intervening." We received the loan in two days, and we decided to put the money toward the rent and car note, which was very important than the other bills. We still were way behind in all the bills. This helped a little bit, but we still were facing a major problem. Even though we paid money on those two bills, we were still way behind on them and other bills.

However, as time went on, I was still feeling hurt and disappointed, and I needed to be in church. I did not have a church home at that time, but I would still consult with my mother who is an overseer (pastor). My mother lives in North Carolina, and I would call her from time to time. I still felt like being in a church home and feeling the presence of God and being ministered to my soul. I was really going through something, and I needed God's guidance and healing. I remember a classmate (Ms. Beth) had offered me to attend her church home (Princeton Church of Christ in Princeton, New Jersey) on several occasions, but I could never get there because things would always come up, and I also would take that time to work on my class assignments on Sundays. I always would stay ahead of my assignments just in case I do not understand, make corrections, and e-mail my professors to overlook my assignment before I send my final paper.

Meanwhile, one day in (August 12, 2017) class, a classmate asked me about coming to her church, and I said, "Yes, I would love to attend your church. It will be my pleasure to visit your church because I was not able to come any other time when you ask me." The classmate said she will call me to confirm my coming and picking me up as well. I was delighted in going because I needed this because of what I'm going through. On August 13, 2017, my classmate came to pick me up for church. As we traveled, we prayed and talked on our way to church. She was very excited in me coming to church, and I was also excited myself.

This was a very special day for me because God prepared a special setup just for me. When I entered the church doors, I was introduced to the pastor who greeted me at the door along with other members. One of the attending ushers or members handed me their program. I went into the church, which was amazing and beautiful all in one word. I felt a lot of love coming from the members as they smiled, shook my hand, and embraced me with their love. As I sat down on the bench and begin to read the program, I noticed the program stated, "Couples Ministry: Attention All Married Couples! You are invited to meet today after worship. Lunch will be provided following a light meal. Pastor Wadzeck will deliver a short message of encouragement." What's so great about it was that the pastor ministered the word in talking about "The Marriage Paradox: Introduction." A paradox consists of statements that lead to an apparent or real contradiction in logic or intuition. God created marriage as a covenant relationship where two distinct individuals become one. The pastor also followed his message behind scriptures such as the following:

A. God created men and women to be coregents over creation as a united force for good.

Genesis 1:27–28

Genesis 2:24

B. Human rebellion against God's will resulted in men and women becoming conflicted and disunited with one another.

Genesis 3:16

Genesis 4:6–7

C. In Christ, our true humanity and individual identity are restored so we can become one in our relationships like marriage.

Ephesians 5:21

Ephesians 5:31–33

Conclusion: Our relationship with God through Christ enables us to become individuals capable of being united with others without losing our identity. Amen.

1 Corinthians 1:10

My God, the Lord knew exactly when I needed to be there out of all the times I kept missing the opportunity to attend my classmate's church. God set up my own schedule, and he did not allow me to miss my appointment. He knew just what my heart needed in going through my marriage and other obstacles in my life. God is greatly to be praised. God is dependable. He is right on time. God works around the clock, 24-7 throughout. Nobody can do it but God.

My classmate said, "What a coincidence that you came on the exact day when my pastor ministered the word on marriage and along with couple ministry workshop." This was the first time on this exact day they set up a couple's ministry workshop for married couples. They were also open to single or those who are planning on getting married or thinking about marrying. The service had really touched my heart; it was a blessing to my soul. My friend Beth was a very supportive person. She called me constantly to pray and read a scripture. She always asked if I am okay and taking the time out to listen. She is an awesome woman of God, and she loves the Lord dearly. I truly thank God for this friend indeed. She also helped me and my husband to get into marriage counseling with her pastor.

We would attend every Thursday for an hour, from four to five in the afternoon. My husband said when I mentioned about the church at the beginning, he would also attend church as well when he gets time or he will take off from work. He also agreed to attend a marriage therapy as well. He said whatever I want, he will do it as well. I prayed to God about talking it over with my husband, and God dealt with the humbleness in his spirit. When we went through our first session, it was okay at first until I broke down and cried in telling the pastor what brought us here in this session. I told the pastor everything that took place in our home. I also said how I was hurt and do not know what to do because we were about to lose everything. I said, "I know you supposed to forgive, but it is hard because it still bothers my heart. I love my husband dearly, but he hurt me. My husband looks at me as if you do not need to let them know everything. The only way to the let the process heal is if we be honest about everything." During the times we were in sessions, we had disagreements because my husband would try to talk over me and interrupting my space and time, which was very rude. My husband was pointing fingers at me and trying to say I was the cause of the problem. He was trying to blame me instead of facing and admitting his own faults because it takes two to argue. I was very upset with him to the point I started to blast him out.

I said, "Speak when you're told to speak. Do not interrupt me because I gave you respect when you were opening. So do not cut me off because you do not like what is being said. I am the type of woman who would speak her mind and would be very defensive when I feel someone is trying to get over on you or tries to put you down." My husband would also say, "You knew what you got yourself into. You knew exactly what type of person I was. If you felt like you did not like what I was doing and not being a good example for your kids, you did not have to continue this relationship." He would come at me in all angles to put shame on me. I would also say, "You knew what type of person I was yourself, and if you felt like I was too much for you and you weren't going to be that role model, you should have bounced. But instead, you were comfortable in what I had to offer someone who had their priorities in order. I gave you my life that included a church girl who had love for you and others, is compassionate, trustworthy, respectful, and had a career, job, education, a family, apartment, car, bank account, and much more. Who would not want to leash off someone else's success when they do not have their own? I love you, and I did not judge your lifestyle. I tried to give you a good life along with me and my family. I think everyone deserves a chance in life regardless of their past. I am not a selfish human being at all, nor do I come to hurt or play with anyone feelings. I can admit to my faults. I fell in love with you because you gave me a steady relationship in my life. You were there for me in ways when I was feeling lonely and empty inside and did not feel loved. I thought you were a different person."

Chapter 8

WHEN THE ENEMY IS AT LARGE, GOD WILL SEE YOU THROUGH YOUR STORM

Note: Men and women, being vulnerable (weak, prone, and helpless), I allowed my emotion and feelings to get the best of me, which shattered my heart. I felt pleased about being in a relationship because he showed me attention by doing everything with me, even though I did everything. His identity was a street thug who had nothing to offer but dishonor, deceit, adultery, cheating, and lies. These were my desires, wants, and needs that came before my face. The unrevealed shadow walker peaked into my life and used my weakness so that I can think that my needs are being satisfied or met. I got comfortable in seeing the good deeds in a person, and I also lost focus on God. We still must keep a focus mind on our God, or we will lose out and be bound to Satan's works. Do not stop praying no matter how it looks and feels.

One cannot put the blame on one person; you must be honest and open about your own dilemmas. This is the only way a relationship can be processed for a complete change of healing. We continued to go to therapy until we could not anymore due to the car situation. We were doing better as we were going to our sessions.

However, speaking about the car situation is another drama. Just when you think it is getting better, it gets worse again. On November

09, 2017, this was when we were getting the clothes together so that we can take it to the laundromat to dry them. The gas was off, so we were not able to cook. There was no heat, no hot water. We were able to wash our clothes with cold water with the colored clothes and white clothes. We were not able to use the dryer in our house due to no heat and no hot water. I bagged up all the clothes that were washed on November 08, 2017, so we can take it to the laundromat the next day, which was November 09, 2017. On that day, we got up to prepare ourselves to dry the clothes at the laundromat. My husband went downstairs to gather up the bags and take them to the car. I started to hear my husband call my name. "Bay, bay, come here," he said. I went to the top of the second stairway to see what the matter was. I said, "Yes, what is wrong?" He said, "The car is gone." I said, "What?" He said, "They came and took the car." I said, "What? Oh no! I just made the payment on the car."

I told my husband I made the payment on November 02, 2017, and I was caught up to one more payment to make. The other payment was not due until the following month. I told my husband also they said if I made the payment before Friday, I would be okay from the repo taking the car. My husband got on the phone and made a call to Nissan Infinite where the payment goes to. The representor came online, and my husband explained the situation. The representor stated that the repo came and took possession of our vehicle due to nonpayment. My husband and I explained again that the payment was paid on November 02, 2017. The representor got another party involved to see where the money was collected at. My husband was speaking to a lady on the phone while the representor was still on the phone. My husband then asked me how I made the payment and when did I made the payment. I stated that I made the payment with my credit card on November 02, 2017, with the representor by the name of Ms. Tanisha. The representor that was handling it said they found what happened. The representor said, "The lady who took your payment and had put it in the wrong account, and that is why the payment was not seen." My husband said, "So it's your fault that they did not see the payment that was made." My husband then went back talking to the first party representor; he said he was going to put us on hold to explain the situation to his supervisor. The representor came back on and stated that they tried to reach us yesterday, and if I had answered the call, this situation would have been avoided. My husband and I stated that this does not make any sense at all. This was ridiculous! It's not our fault that they did not receive the payment due to their error. We asked to speak to the supervisor. We did not get nowhere our problem at all. She kept on repeating the same thing: if we had responded to them calling us, this would have been resolved. I was heated up and told my husband this was so wrong. My husband continued to speak to the supervisor. Then he ended the conversation. He told me she gave him the information to where the car is at, how much we needed to get the car back, along with three references. I said, "Who got that kind of money. It isn't okay. My car is just gone." My husband kept saying, "I am so sorry I put you into this situation, babe."

I left it alone because there was not anything that I could do. I felt very hurt and helpless in this situation. I am so glad that I serve a great God. My sister called me later that day. I was very depressed. I explained to my sister that my car was gone, and I was hurting. She said, "OMG, trust me, sis. I understand." I stated that the representor Ms. Tanisha placed my payment in the wrong account, which made them not aware of the payment that was made on November 02, 2017. They said they tried to reach out to me yesterday, and if I had answered the call, this would have been avoided. It was $534 paid to them due to an error on their behalf. My sister told me to give her all the information on the gas bill and truck and she will call to speak to someone for me in the morning. I have a smart and business-minded sister. She does not stand for nonsense at all. She works for investor bank and been working there now for about nineteen or twenty-two years. She is a supervisor who knows about business hardcore. She will challenge you to the end and come out successful in Jesus's name. If she feels like she is not getting anywhere with you, she will go over your head to a higher authority. I am the exact same way in any situation that I may face. My sister went out her way for me especially on this day of her anniversary. My sister husband took me and my husband to the laundromat on the same day. We had a busy day.

However, my sister called the next morning as she stated, on November 10, 2017. She told me to be praying because she was waiting for the manager to call her back. She also said the board of utilities was out of the office today, so she left a voice message. On November 03, 2017, I spoke to the renter's office concerning my rent, which they indicated that they will be sending me out a court date to come to court regarding my rent being three months behind. They also stated that if I pay it before I meet my court date, they will disregard my court date. They posted in the letter as a notice November 03, 2017, on a Friday, and the court date on December 06, 2017, was for me to meet in court. However, I was so worried and did not know what to do. My mother kept saying, "Do not worry. God is going to make a way." I kept on praying every day with my mother and reading the Word. I never gave up even though worries would creep up on me from time to time. My mother came to me one day and said, "Do you trust God?" I said yes. She said, "Do you trust him all the way to the fullest?" I said, "I trust God but sometimes I feel a little worried, but I know God will help me." My mother said, "I ask you that question because God told me to tell you to trust him all the way. That means there is no doubt or worry that should be in the midst of you trusting God. If you believe he will bring you out, that means you have faith in God knowing that he is going to take care of your situation.

Note: We may go through a few unpleasant, bad relationships

and marriage, but if you go deep down in your soul and let strength come up to the surface, you can overcome those heavy loads. There just challenges that we may face to see how we are going to come out in overcoming those hardships. I believe it comes only to make us stronger in dealing with obstacles. This will allow us to be aware of growing a good sense of knowledge and being familiar with what we dealt with in our life. However, when it comes around again, you will quietly in your spirit be on point on how to deal with the familiar things that you have encountered. With God's grace and mercy, endure it all to let the heavy weight fall off. There's power in the name of Jesus.

I remember on November 10, 2017. I came downstairs to pray by myself because sometimes God will lead me to pray alone. I was sitting in the chair, meditating on God and saying, "What am I going to do, God? I cannot be put out of my house. I cannot see me and my son put out with nowhere to go and giving up on school as well." Then God spoke to me and said, "Call your oldest son and ask him for the money." I said, "My son, God? I do not want to ask him because I do not feel like explaining and going into detail and especially just hearing my son complaining." I told God I'm not in the mood for lecture, or I could never ask my son for money because I was always the type of mother who would always give to my sons, especially if they need anything.

God spoke again, "Call your son. He has the money, and he can afford to help you." I then obeyed God and I said, "I am going to text because he probably is at work." I texted this: "Gm. Jaquan I really need a favor from you regarding money. I can give it back once my money come in about three weeks." Soon as I texted my son, he immediately called me back within seconds. He said, "Mom, what you need? I got money." I said, "I needed the money to get caught back up for my rent, and Kevin no longer has his jobs." He said, "Mom, I know what happened. You do not have to explain nothing to me. If you need money, it is no problem. You are my mother. Of course I would want to help you out. Money is nothing to me especially if you need my help." He asked me how much, and I said, "Eight hundred." He said, "How soon you need it?" I said, "Next week." He said, "Okay, I got you." Then we hung up, and then I texted my son, "Thank you so very much." My son texted back, "You're welcome. That's what family is for. Just need it back. LOL. That is out of my savings account. Sure that is all you need though?" My son is a joker; he always made people laugh. I texted, "If you can give extra, I really appreciate it." It was kind of funny to me that even though I said I needed eight hundred, I was thinking about extra, but I did not want to go overboard. Then my son texted back, "Sure, that's all you need tho."

My son texted again, "I send a thousand." I was so happy, and I texted him, "I really appreciate it." The heaviness was off my heart right then. I would most definitely give it back and extra for you and the baby that was on the way. On November 13, 2017, my son's girlfriend sent the money. I texted my son again, "OK. Thank you again, son, for your help. You will get it back and more." My son texted, "I told you no problem. Just take care of your business. Welcome." On November 15, 2017, I texted my son, "Good afternoon. Thank you very much, son. I just paid the rent off and got a few groceries a well." My son texted "OK. If you need to hold some more money, let me know. But you're welcome anytime." I want to thank my heavenly Father for his help in seeing to my needs. He will never fail you. He is a right-on-time God, and I am so grateful for his hands. I also want to thank both of my sons for their help in seeing to their mother's needs.

On November 11, 2017, who would have known that this was going to be the last day I would see my husband. A classmate of mine picked me and my son up from my house to go to school. I told my classmate about my situation of not having my vehicle anymore, and they jumped right in and said, "We got you." While at school on my lunch break, my husband sent me a text about 2:03 p.m. saying, "Hey, bay, call me soon as you get out of class. It's important." I immediately called him, and he answered, "Oh, bay, you did not have to call me right now because I know you are at school. I did not want to disturb you while you in class. You could've call me when you got out." I said, "What is the problem?" He said, "My job at BJs called me to come in, and it was important. I told them whatever they had to say, they can tell me now because I do not want to waste money on a cab to come out there for nothing." He continued, "The manager said that he was terminating me due to no shows and lateness." I said, "We already knew that they were going to let you go because you missed too many days by calling out. I have to go now." He said, "Okay, we can talk more about when you get home." I said, "Okay. Love you." I also told my husband I brought him and my son some food. I was thinking about him eating, so I took the few dollars that I had and spent it to get food for them. My husband had lost both jobs at that time. This was really a heavy load right now for me again.

When I arrived home, my husband was standing in the garage with the garage door up as my classmate pulled up in my driveway. I got out of the car, but I was noticing how my husband looked off. This puzzled me for a second, but I brushed it off like it was nothing. I said hello to my husband and went straight upstairs to my room to put my things away. My husband then came upstairs to talk to me. He stated that he needed to leave and go and make some money by selling his illegal product. I most definitely disapprove of that kind of activity. He also said, "I need to do something because I just cannot sit here and do nothing at all. We need the money so we can get out of the situation that I caused." I said, "There is a better way than that. I am sorry, but I just cannot accept that at all. This is not me at all, and I refuse to be a part of such activity. We just need to figure out another way than this. God knows the situation. He can bring us out if we just try him. He did it before, and he can most definitely do it again." God does not want us to go a step ahead of him; he wants us to fall back behind him so that he can work his glory of favors, healing, and blessings for us. If we tend to move ahead of God, we just set ourselves up for disappointments. We will end up causing the situation to get worse than what it was already. Why cause damages to the scenery more if we can avoid the corruption by allowing God to pull us out of the difficult situations. We allow our eagerness, selfishness, or know-it-all self to intervene in the wrong way that will put us in more harmful debts. My husband said, "You just do not understand. I need to do this. Can you please listen to me? I am trying to explain this is what I want to do. I know you do not approve of this, babe, and I do understand your feelings. This is something I want to do, whether you agree or disagree." I just stood by the bed, silent with thoughts running through my head saying, "I cannot believe this is happening." My husband then said, "I have to go. Give me a kiss, and I will be back so I can help you with your PowerPoint and get the letter from my job so you can take it to Section 8." I did not move. I just stared at him, and then I brushed it off by turning my head toward a different direction. My husband then said, "You going to feel sad and regret it if something would happen to me and you didn't kiss me. You love me. You're going to feel really hurt." I was then startled (shocked and remorseful) about what he said. So I went to kiss my husband. Then he said, "Do you still have the food for me that you bought?" I was a little upset at this situation that was taking place I didn't even want to give him the food at all because he was leaving me instead of staying and handling this situation in a more positive and productive manner.

    I gave my husband the food, and we went downstairs. He went into the kitchen to eat, and I sat down in the living room. My husband had finished up eating and then came into the living room to give me a kiss goodbye. He said he loves me. He went downstairs, and my son came up to let me know about going to ShopRite to get food. My mother gave me her credit card, and I told my son I was coming. I got up to go put my coat on from the closet. I looked downstairs at my brother-in-law and said, "Why are you looking at me like that? You do not want me to go?" He said, "I do not have a problem with it." I went downstairs and proceeded out the front door. I got into the car and my husband got in. I was thinking why he was getting in the car. I was puzzled. My brother-in-law was taking him to the train station. I thought he was taking an Uber. My husband reached over to give me a kiss and said he will call me later. He got out of the vehicle to get his belongings out the truck of the car. Then he asked my brother-in-law if he has change. He said no. Then he looked at me and said, "I only have enough of money when I get out there to my destination." He said, "I would have given you money if I had extra." I just looked away and thought about how he is going to give him money after I took my last dime to buy him food to eat. I forgot he got paid. If I had remembered, I would have approached him about it. However, my husband knew I did not have any money. He even knew the situation in the household. My husband left that night at the train station. I never knew that it was going to be the last time I see his face.

Chapter 9

RED FLAG—GOD IS STILL IN CONTROL

On November 13, 2017, my sister texted me and said she spoke to Mr. Garfield about the situation about my car and he was straightening it out on the strength of my youngest sister. My vehicle was returned on November 14, 2017. I was glad, but I was still worried because of making the payments ($400 a month). I did not have that kind of money, especially I'm living on Social Security. My husband was gone and doing whatever he pleased. I called my husband and told him they returned the vehicle back, and he said, "That is good." My husband and I got into an argument because I said, "Why are you sounding different?" He was talking about things that did not make any sense, trying to blame me suddenly and saying he does not know when he was coming back home. I got upset and went off. After I calmed down, I texted my husband, "Love you, babe. I'm so scared for you. That's why I keep praying for God to touch your situation." My husband texted "I understand, bay, and I know you want me home also. But I just have to see where this road takes me. And even though I believed it is somewhere bad, I know it is a big chance that it might be. And if so, then I will just have to accept the consequences.

But right now, I feel like this is where I am meant to be. Doing what I am doing. I just really need money right now, bay. Tired of working myself to death for nothing. I know I'm capable of starting and running my own successful business. I just need the right amount of money to do it. And I know I am not going to get it from simply working. No, you do not agree, but I just hope you understand. I love you so much, bay. But I must do this for me, so one day, I can really take care of you, like you deserve."

My husband had his own agenda, and I was not included in it. When he left me on November 11, 2017, he knew he was not going to come back. He left me in a bad state, which he had created. He caused a dilemma in our family. How can a man have it in his heart to abandon his wife at a state of a bad hardship? All the problem was left on me to deal with, and I was so angry. It was so bad that we have no hot water and were washing up in cold water at the sink. Never in my life had I imagined washing up in cold water. To feel that coldness touching your face and private parts. I had to get used to taking these cold washes. One day, it was so cold, the water felt like icicle. But then, it dawned on me to warm the water up in the microwave, so practically from time to time, I would heat the water up in the microwave for my mother and me. I wanted to make sure my mother was good.

I had to take on all these problems and realized there was not any other choices to a better solution. One day, while I was washing up, I looked in the mirror and said, "I deserve better than this." There was no food to eat. I had to go to the food bank to get food, didn't have money to dry our clothes, and ended up hanging it around the house. There was no heat, but thank God, I had the two heaters to keep us warm, one heater I kept up stairs and one downstairs. It was amazing they did not cut my lights off, so I thank God. I could not cook on the stove. We did have a little money, along with the help of my baby sister. We would buy cooked food and cold cuts and other items that we were able to eat. My sister did not have a place of residence. She and her husband were living from hotel to hotel, and she ended up living with me couple of times till she got enough of money up and left. Even though she had her own struggles, she still was supportive in a lot of ways toward my needs.

One day, I came downstairs because I didn't know what we

were going to eat, and my amazing mother had a full course meal she cooked in the microwave. I never thought about using the microwave like that. She made macaroni and cheese, mashed potatoes, yellow and white rice, sweet candy yams, the box of stuffing, and vegetables. The meat was cooked in a crock pot that my mother gave me as a Christmas present. It came in handy, and also we ate oatmeal for breakfast. My mother said, "Anything that says microwave, you can cook in a microwave. God will make a way in being a provider. I was born and raised in the country I know how to survive."

My husband and I would text each other:

November 13, 2017.

(husband) Love you babe. Call you soon as I get a chance. Promise (smiley face). 2:25 a.m.

(wife) I am sorry I was agitated. Love you so much, babe. 2:13 p.m.

(husband) Love you too. I will call you later 2:19 p.m.

(wife) Okay. 3:52 p.m.

November 14, 2017

(wife) Love you babe. I am so scared for you. That is why I keep praying for God to touch your situation. 1:58 p.m.

(husband) I understand, bay, and I know you want me home also. But I just must see where this road takes me. And even though I believe it is not somewhere bad. I know it is a big chance that it might be. And if so, then I will just have to accept the consequences. But right now, I feel like this is where I am meant to be, doing what I am doing. I just really need $money$ right now, bay. Tired of working myself to death for nothing. I know I can start my own successful business. I just need the right amount of money to do it. And I know I am not going to get it from simply working. No, you do not agree. But I just hope you understand. I love you so much bay. But I must do this for me. So one day I can really take care of you, like you deserve. (emojis, kisses, faces, and hearts)

This is nothing but babbling words of a joker. Taking care of me was showing me a strong man that can stand as a soldier and fighting through the battlefield in any circumstance until victory was won. It is not copping out when you cannot stand the heat or bailing out and throwing up the flag and giving up on your family. Especially when you caused all of it and left them behind for someone else to clean it up. My god. You are in it to win it together.

November 18, 2017

(wife) Good morning, babe. Love you. I am at school in Jesus's name. God bless. (emojis praying hands, peace sign, and a smiley face) 7:34 p.m.

(husband) Good morning to you too. Sorry I did not call you back last night. Got caught up in some stuff. Have a good day in school. Love you too 1:15 p.m.

November 20, 2017

(husband) Called BJs. She said she must look for the paperwork. Then call me back. Then I will call or text you. 4:02 p.m.

November 21, 2017

(husband) Go to BJs when you ever get a chance. They have a folder for you. With the papers you need. Ask for Audrina. 1:08 p.m.

Note: This paper was what I needed to take to Section 8 stating that my husband was not no longer employed so that the rent can be decreased. He was giving me a pretty hard time getting it for me. He told me to take him off the lease because he did not want to get unemployment and work.

November 21, 2017

(wife) I am in a meeting right now 1:09 p.m. (husband) Okay, just letting you know. It is there

waiting. Probably should pick it up some time today. 1:31 p.m.

(wife) Okay. I love you too. I will call you later 5:42 p.m.

(husband) Okay, bay, I really do love you. Even though right now it does not seem like it. But love is not our issue. Love is the reason why we made it so far. I just really needed some time away to figure out who I really am. And what I really want in life. And I could not do it being there. But I know you do not understand that. Because you are blessed to know exactly who you are. I always had to be the bad guy growing up. Then I meet you, and you were so good to me. Giving and loving. And I really tried to be a good guy for you. But I am really starting to see that that is not who I am. I am a bad guy. Always have been and probably always will be. We're married so you know I am not going nowhere. You just have to accept who and what I am. I am a bad guy. And the days of me pretending that I am good is over 6:23 p.m.

The unrevealing shadow walker in a human being form has revealed his identity.

November 21, 2017

(wife) I am here trying to figure out how to handle some things, and it is not right at all. I would never leave someone in a dilemma like this. This is not cool at all. I do not have gas on in the house and among other things that is going on as well. This is very hurtful right now. You're trying to figure out things in a warm home with everything else is going well for you. That is not love at all. I do not have money to eat really. I cannot get up and leave and walk away if I wanted to, but somehow, some way, God will help heal my heart because he knows this is wrong. This is not what marriage supposed to be. God says for better or for worse and for rich and poor. You said you are trying to find yourself, and you were made to be a bad person, but sometimes even the baddest person still has a conscience and a good heart to do what is right. My mother is here, and it hurts me to let my mother see me like this, especially when the man was supposed to do right by her daughter. I never seen or expect this to happen to me like this way 9:29 p.m.

(wife) This really took me by surprise. I never would have treated you like this at all. I never gave you any cruel ways of being dishonest or disrespecting you in dealing with a man or calling a man. I was so faithful to you in all aspect of our marriage. We were supposed to depend on each other no matter what life comes against us. You're good because you're living a double life that is away from home. I will rise, and trust me, I may cry or shed a couple of tears, but God will make me whole again. Love you always from my heart. 9:36 p.m.

November 22, 2017

(wife) Happy Thanksgiving and be safe. I love you very much 9:39 a.m.

(husband) I love you too, bay. Happy Thanksgiving, and I will try my best to be safe 11:20 a.m.

On this morning, I decided to text my husband, still feeling hurt but still having a heart. My mother, my son and I went to my sister's place, at the hotel she was staying at to have Thanksgiving and wash up. We brought the food we cooked to go along what she had as well. I arrived at the hotel and brought my belongings in and sat it down. My mother said, "Go ahead and wash up." I said, "I know, Mom, you do not have to tell me. I know when to go and wash up." I felt a certain way when my mother made that statement because my mind went, "I cannot believe I have to take shower over to someone's else place." I have not taken a shower in days, just bird bath at the sink (cold water). I felt like a homeless person trying to get by to survive. Meanwhile, I did not look at it like that because this was my sister's place. I looked at it as being brought down to humiliation.

I went with my belongings into the bathroom and placed them on top of the sink. I investigated the mirror, and I broke down with tears. My sister came in the bathroom and shut the door and hugged me and said, "It is going to be all right, sister." I said, "I cannot believe he did this to me. I never treated him like this. I did so much for him and everybody else. Why I must be mistreated? This is not love at all. This hurts bad, and I do not wish this on nobody because pain is very hurtful to the heart." My sister said, "I can't say I understand because I never experienced what you're going through, but I do know God is going to deal with Kevin because he made a vow to you and God. God sees what is going on, and Kevin cannot get away with it. You do not hurt a person and move on and think you are not going to reap what you sow. You belong to God. I know this is hurting you, sis. But when it is all over, you are going to help a lot of people."

I cried so hard, and the bad thing about it was when you are with someone for so many years, it is hard to detach yourself from that individual. God took his time and worked on my heart and spirit.

November 23, 2017

(wife) I have to call you back 2:26 p.m.

Babe I will call you in a minute 2:27 p.m. I was calling you back 3:04 p.m.

(husband) I know, bay. I'm a call you in a few.

Love you. (smiley face) 3:12 p.m. (wife) Love you too. 3:18 p.m.

That is okay. Do not bother to call me back. It's all good. Hope you are enjoying your family feast 5:01 p.m.

(husband) All you do is show me attitude. If you wanted me to come home so bad, maybe you will be nice about it. Try a little sweet talk. But you're incapable of being nice about things. Always got to be so hard about everything. You ever heard the saying you can catch more flies with honey than vinegar. God, why you always must be so aggressive 9:43 p.m.

(wife) You're so wrong about the way you are talking to me. You want me to beg you. Yeah right. I do not even have money to eat. My family trying their best to support me, which is your job. I have a right to be upset about everything that is going on. You are the one is treating me wrong. It is okay. Party on, babe. 10:05.

November 25, 2017

(husband) You said to not bother to call you. So I guess I will wait for you to call me. Just know I am always thinking about you. Watch "New Edition—I'm still in love with you" on YouTube https://youtu.be/RT1MAzyUkJE 3:31 p.m.

I did not call my husband in the last two days after he made that comment on November 22, 2017. So I guess he decided to respond when he did not hear from me. I read the text, and then I listened to the song, and I forgot I was upset with him.

November 25, 2017

(wife) I will call you tonight, babe. I really miss you, and I love you very much 3:48 p.m.

That song was beautiful, babe 4:41 p.m. It really touched my spirit 4:41 p.m.

(husband) Please, bay, just give me some time to figure it things out. I am really lost right now. And I cannot find myself being there right now. And I know with the financial situation. This is a horrible time to leave. But I know everything happens for a reason. I been feeling like we needed some time apart. But I could not force myself to leave you, but circumstance causes us to do. What we do not have the strength to do ourselves. Anyway. Looking forward to your call. I will talk to you later. Miss you and love you always 4:25 p.m.

 My husband left me in a state of a terrible situation with no regrets. He knew all along he was leaving and did not have the guts to tell me in my face. He caused all this headache and hardship on me and moved on like nothing to it with no remorse. Oh! But he loves me, and he needs time to think. He said, "I am tired of working. I do not know what I want." He said all this when the gas was off, with no food to eat, rent backed up/evicted, and car was taken. I said, "You're living with a friend in a nice, comfortable house with hot running water, eating good, money in your pocket, and a vehicle to drive." All the times my husband did not pay the bills, he was saving it for his own selfish self. My husband had a plan that was to destroy me in bringing me down to nothing. He once told me, "You would know now how it feels to have nothing, and this will make you get off your lazy butt and get a job now and use your degrees. You always had everything in life, so see how you get yourself out of this by yourself." Note: My husband never mentioned about the story he told about owning money to the gang members, the Bloods (paying his supposed-to-be debt off). If I owe a debt especially to a gang member and I lose both of my jobs, I would be furious, scared, fear for my life and family, or have panic attacks. I would not leave my family behind and start a new life over by myself. When people tell stories, their action must be connected to their story. Evidence will show and tell you whether it is real or not. He said they had our address. They would have attempt to come to our residence and make some noise (figure of speech). It never happened because it was a lie. My husband never paid the bills because he saved up the money to leave and start his own journey of a life with his new mistress. When people do wrong things toward innocent people or people in general, the truth always shows up, and that person will cause hardship on their own life for hurting people. They always say that God does not like ugly behavior.

 This was a hard situation for me and having my mother there

as well to see this entire situation taking place with her daughter. I never, in my life, imagined myself facing this kind of hardship at all. I cried out to my mother and said, "I am sorry you had to see this happening to me and suffering along with me." My mother said to me, "It is all right. I know this is not your fault. I am here for you to help you get through this situation. I came up for the funeral, but I know now I had to be here for you. God knows everything, and he knew what you were going to face. That is why he knew I had to be here, not for the funeral, but for you as well. We are going to be all right because we got God. The most amazing favor of God, our resource like no other."

My husband called me on November 30, 2017, which was one of the most devastating situations I had to face being as a wife. I had just left from an appointment around 1:00 p.m. at that time. My husband said, "Babe, I have to talk to you about something that is very important." At that time, I was on my way to my therapist, which has grown into a good friendship. I said, "What is it? Is it bad?" He said, "I do not know how to tell you." I said, "You seeing someone?" He said no. I asked, "You got a disease or living with a female?" He said he was drinking bad when he was over to his friend's house and slept with this female. He also said his friends shared the same female as well. He did not find out until one day, he was talking and bragging about this female he slept with to his friends. His friends turned around and said how they slept with the same female as well. I said, "You talk about it with your friends like it was not nothing but a joke and started to laugh about it with them. When they mentioned about sleeping with the same female, then it got very skeptical to you, so now you decided to tell me now." My husband said that same night he slept with the female, he came home and lay with me. I knew something was not right that night because it was the way he was having intimacy with me. It felt different. I said, "You just got through lying with a female and came and lay with me? Seriously? You ungrateful bastard. You nasty, dirty, and filthy human being!" He said, "I needed to get myself checked out because she has been lying around with other guys." Then he said, "I feel fine." I said, "What's that supposed to mean? Just because you feel fine does not say anything at all." He said, "I just wanted you to get checked out because I know you always go to the doctor."

I screamed out loud and started yelling, "What? I have kids, my mom, and family! I cannot believe you did this to me! This is so wrong!" He said, "That is why I rather you be home than out because I know how you can get." I said, "The blood of Jesus."

Chapter 10

WHEN YOU FEEL RUINED, HOPE AND VICTORY SHALL ARRIVE

Note: Listen, people. This is another Trixie (trick) that the enemy uses. When a man or woman knows you're faithful and keeps up with doctor's appointments in showing good health, they will use your body to see if something is wrong health-wise by sleeping with you after they have committed adulty or infidelity. They figure they would not have to go get checkups because you will be the result of it being negative or positive. You are their guinea pig.

I always used to say to my husband, "I am not feeling good," "Why am I itchy a lot down below?" "Why I am hurting there?" "My stomach is painful," "Why I am irritated?" I would do this to see his reactions. His face would look puzzled, and he will get quiet. Then he would say, "I do not know. You have to go to the doctor or let me see." He will also go to the store to pick up pain pills or ask if I called the doctor yet.

Then he flipped the script and started blaming me:

    A. My son and I were always riding around in the car using it, and he has to pay for it.

    B. I always question him about paying the bills.

    C. I do not cook or clean.

D. I never was there for him at all. I was not supportive.

E. I am selfish and only think about myself, and we were always arguing.

This is what a cruel person would say, instead of taking the blaming for their own action. I never was about mistreating anyone wrong or being cruel to them. This is not my character, but yes, I do have a heart. I am a good woman, and yes, I flip out on him out of anger. I cried with anger. I said, "Nigger, you are not the only one that pays bills. From day one, I have been paying bills and still is, and my son pays part too. Just because you started working for a couple of years now, you are getting ahead of yourself. You as a husband has a responsibility to take care of your family. You were not complaining for years when I was doing everything and taking care of your family, while on top of that, I still paying bills and in school. I have cooked, praying for you, preparing your lunch for work and dinner, telling you I love you, encouraging you, saying how handsome and smart you are, cleaning and washing your clothes, paid for trips, gave my body, made sure you had money in your pocket, gave more on special occasions, and much more. I treated you well then and now. We both pay the bills in this house, so do not get it twisted."

He was being mean on the phone after he done told me he slept

with a female. I got off the phone and went into the office with my therapist. I just broke down and cried so hard. I explained what happened and said, "People think they're really going to get away with hurting someone. I belong to a God who loves me very much, and I know how to pray up above heaven.:

I remember coming home with a heavy weight on my mind. I immediately called and made an appointment. I told my husband I made an appointment and asked him was he coming with me to the doctor. His statement was, "I do not think I am able to come." I said, "What? You are not coming to the doctor with me?" He said, "I do not want to make any promises and say yes, and do not come." I said, "How are you going give someone news like that and do not be there for them. You are the cause of it, and you are just going to let me face it by myself." On August 6, 2018, I broke down again just by telling it. Still brings me so much pain and hurt. I never spoke with him since then.

December 05, 2017 was my appointment to see the OB/GYN. On that day, my mother came with me to the doctor. She was always my supporter through thick and thin. My doctor came in the examining room, cheerful as always. He said, "What brings you in today?" I explained to the doctor why I was there: due to my husband's statement of how he slept with this female who slept with his friends as well. He also left his marriage, and I need to get tested. I said, "I wanted to get tested for everything and including my pap smear. My doctor stated that he could not do both test due to my insurance, so I must do one today and come back in two days to take the other test. As I was talking, I just started crying because of hurt, embarrassment, and anger. I just could not believe the fact I was sitting in the doctor's office, getting tested because my husband committed adultery by messing around with females. My mother said, "What are you crying for? You do not need to cry. You're going to be okay." The doctor felt my pain and said, "I have some equipment right here that I can check and test right quick and take your blood work. You still can come in the next day or two to do the pap smear." So he examined me with some tool and looked through this device to check and see if my wall has been ruptured or broken. However, he took whatever and ran a quick test and said he did not see anything that indicated any signs of symptoms. Then he told me to come back for my blood work results in two weeks. I came back to do the last test pap smear and waited two weeks to come back for the results.

I remember talking to a good close friend, Pastor Linda (classmate). She encouraged my heart. She even told me about her situation with her first husband and about a friend who died. She told me her husband was a drug user; he would stay away from home for days and weeks. He would spend his paycheck and leave his family in situation of not being able to eat and provide things for the children's personal needs. She also told me that her husband ended up having AIDS. She said one day, she had a phone call to come in and get tested. She told the doctor that she was not coming in because she knows God and she is fine. She stood her ground and trusted God's unchanging hands. She said she belongs to God who was her protector. Her husband died, and she was clear from all disease. She also got remarried and continued to stay in the will of God. She said, "If you belong to God, he will not prevent any harm and danger to come up against you."

She is a prayer warrior and God's anointed prophetess. She told me to trust God, which was a confirmation, and to believe that God was on my side. She told me to hold on because he knows the heart and the situation. She gave me a scripture to read. And a song by Tamela Mann "Through It All" is very encouraging. She was such a blessing to me so much. God put people in your life at the right time because he sees far ahead to know what is going to take place. She is a strong tower, a faith believer, and does not take or accept the enemies' mess.

I remember waiting to go in for my test results. I was so worried, very quiet, sad, and I was barely eating. I prayed a lot and cried constantly in my own secret closet in my bedroom. My mother said, "I see a big word over you that says trust in gold writing. God wants you to trust him. That means when you give it to him, you must believe it's done. Do not worry yourself about it. Let go and rest in God." She also said that God let her know that my husband has been with more than one woman. I told my mother my husband was going to reap what he sowed. However, weeks went past (three weeks), and I missed my appointment. I was rescheduled to come in on December 22, 2017, to find out my test results. On that day, I was a little nervous, and he was very busy that day too because I was waiting forever in the examining room. My mother and my youngest son were there with me at the doctor's office, but my mother did not come in the room.

The doctor eventually came in the room and said, "A few jokes and apologies for having me waiting for a very long time. So why are you here?" I am looking like really. I said I came for the test results. He said, "Okay, so get dressed and meet me in my office." There was an intern in his office, and he asked me was it okay for him to sit because of his training. I said it was fine and congratulations. The doctor looked at my results on his screen and said, "Mrs. Hardy, everything came back normal. You're fine. If it were not, you would have been called, so you do not have to worry. Your test results came back good, and I see you next year for your annual check all over again." I was in tears. My heart was at ease, and all I can say in the office was, "Thank you, God, for covering me, Jesus." Don't be afraid or second-guess yourself of what God can do for you as your provider.

"You just must continue to stay forever at God's feet" by Tasha Cobbs's "Forever at Your Feet."

"God will always take care of his faithful vessel. Let God have his way in your life" by Erick David Townsend's "Psalmist Raine and Refresh." A beautiful healing song.

As LeAndria Johnson said in her songs, "I found me another lover whose name Jesus is. He gives me a knew reasons to stay alive. All the stuff I been through and now I am at a better place." The song is entitled "No More Tears."

My God has "Open Heaven" by Maranda Curtis.

As I say to my Father above heaven, "Father I Belong to You" by Leon Timbo.

"God says if I'm before you who can be against you" (Isaiah 46:4)

I got married to be bonded or tied with the one I love and that my body was to be protected and secured under my husband as well as his body under me. The body of two in a marriage are as one in the body of Christ says the Lord. The husband and the wife's body are no longer their own once they are joined in marriage, which means his body and her body are not to be distribute freely to no one else outside of that marriage.

The word of God, Nerveless, because of sexual immorality, let each man have his own wife, and let each woman have her own husband. Let the husband render to his wife the affection due her, and likewise also the wife to her husband. The wife does not have authority over her own body, but the husband does. And likewise, the husband does not have authority over his own body, but the wife does. (1 Corinthians 7:2–4)

The husband and wife must realize that once a person delivers themselves to someone other than their spouse, they have just broken covenant. What I meant by that is adding a third party that should not have been added to the marriage. You just made it a triple double. Anything or whatever can take place of causing destruction in the marriage because of what you allowed to enter in your home through marriage. That man and woman have to realize they are thinking for two, not one such as, if the man's decision is to fall short, he just made the same decision for both or spoken for both parties because now he's just carrying back to his other half (a sin he picks up) the third (secret or hidden) partner. The same for the wife when it comes to her other half. There was not any protection, covenant, or security for both partners in marriage. When he or she becomes intimate (sex) with a stranger, also enter his or her spouse.

The two as a whole is now a three as a screw up because of one spouse's lust (sin fidelity or a two-face sinner or faithless sinner mix with a righteousness fidelity or loyalty) are now the three musketeers or more (multi-musketeers). The unfaithful spouse's unpleasant aroma, distinctive personality behavior became a deception, sneakiness, selfishness, promise-breaking, debt problems, flirting, always believes there the smartest person then you are, name-calling when upset, blaming others when things go wrong or you the reason why they haven't succeed in life, disregards for other feelings when it conflicts with their own wishes, violent behavior, threats to leave if you don't like it or accept, behaves differently in different company, causing confusing, argumenta, lying, distance, verbal abusive, separation, lack of love, no communication, being overprotective with their cellphones, excess drinking of alcohol, late nights at their job or working overtime, making excuses, comparing you to other woman's or men, change of pattern, and lack of intimacy.

This so sweet aroma scent is now a sour and dreadful scent in the marriage. A married man or a woman can be one way at home and another way from home. A man can play his part so well as a married man in wearing his ring so faithfully, but once he has entered outside of his home, he shows another identity of being an unfaithful spouse (the hidden ring of bondage). He tends to live a double life by leading two separate and very different lives.

However, the day I mention about my appointment date to my husband, which he made an excuse not to come to the doctor, I stopped responding to his texts. I was still going through a tough time, and I was lost, because I have grown so attached to him. It may sound crazy especially after everything that he has done and put his wife through. I started talking to God about everything such as where is my life going at or is this marriage at an end. I don't want to do anything out of God's will, without his direction. I asked God to help my mind and heart. I do honor my marriage, but this is far too much. Why is this happening? I treat and do good from my heart. I give from the kindness of my heart. I don't deserve to be treated this way, and he showed so much hatred and jealousy. This was not how a marriage was supposed to be at all. I know their ups and downs but there are certain limits.

Chapter 11

GOD WILL USE ILLUSTRATIONS TO SHOW THE POWER OF LOVE, WHICH BRINGS HELP AND HEALING WHEN FACING OUR STORM

I remember Apostle Glover told me about a man in the Bible name Hosea. God told him to marry a prostitute by the name of Gomer. God told Hosea to love a woman who was loved by another man and is in adulteress, even as the Lord loves the children of Israel. God commanded Hosea to marry a wife of whoredom. In this, the wife was made holy through the union of a holy prophet, a man of God. I mentioned to the apostle how can I be with my husband who stepped out of our marriage and several other things. I was not giving my body back to a man who commits adultery. Then she told me a short story about Hosea who God told him to marry a prostitute. She said the woman was a prostitute and was married. God used a holy man of God to marry her, and through the whole time, he lived a righteous life before Gomer. This was what change her life, and she became saved. Hosea kept focusing on God and speaking what was righteous before his wife. A sanctified man sanctifies his wife. Hosea was a holy man of God who married an unsaved woman.

God shifted Hosea's own life and marriage into a living moral lesson or parable so that the people of God can catch sight of and testify or give evidence about God's work out of love.

God used Hosea and Gomer (Hosea 1:3) to serve as a dramatic picture (illustration). For this reason, therefore, Gomer was constantly cheating on her husband (Hosea). God then sent Hosea back to retrieve his wife, Gomer.

Gomer was redeemed back on the account of an everlasting or relentless love of her spouse (Hosea). The creator love never stops, never gives up, or never looks for a way out because God's love never fails it is beyond all measures.

Can we question our life to say are you a Hosea or Gomer? If so, the message above gave a good example of how their marriage was a chaos of one spouse by the name of Gomer who kept on time after time committing adultery. God used their life issues for the world to see people have downfalls or circumstances in their marriage, but God did a massive turn around to show love can conquer anything.

God used Prophet Hosea as one who was obedient, stayed faithful, didn't give up, prayed, and continue to show love. Hosea could have bailed out or flee from the scene, but God kept him right there in his circumstances. God refused to let the man of God leave.

This was because God's assignment for Hosea was to be a picture of his amazing love and faithfulness to the people of Israel who failed short in not giving back fidelity (loyalty) to God. Hosea never gave up on his wife at all. Hosea was the example of God. People don't let the negative view out way the good potential stored inside that individual. The Lord gives everyone a chance to redeem themselves back to Christ. God heal their marriage and the people of Israel mind, heart, and soul to salvation. God's love worked through Hosea spiritually until his wife and the people of Israel life were spiritually healed.

Who am I? I am Hosea, and you may be a Hosea. However, some maybe a Gomer, but God still helps no matter what position you are living in. It will always ball down to every soul are counted for a redemption, miracles, or healing of God.

Apostle Glover told me to focus on God, get a church home so I can work for the Lord, connect to the prayer line, listen to gospel music, call up saints of God to pray with me and so that I can be strengthened and do what God asked of me to do. She said, "Do not worry about your husband. Put him in God's hands and keep yourself in the will of God and perform the works of God."

I continued to pray for my heart and my marriage. My family told me to move on with my life and not worry about my husband because he's in God's hands. It was wrong how he treated me and left me deal with issues he accumulated. It was so easy for a person to tell me to move on when they never faced the situation or even know how it really felt to be stripped and left abandoned by your own husband. It was an ongoing pain inside and out.

I remember praying in my secret closet again and God led me to call a good friend of the family, a prophetess. The Lord said, "She was going to give you a word." I have not reached out to her in a long time. I saw her on my Facebook. She was always speaking at other ministries. I decided to call her. She said, "Hi, Catherine, how is your mom? Tell her I said hello and give me call." I said, "Can you pray for me? I need prayer right now." She said, "I'm usually at my office working, but today I decided to stay and work from home and you called at a good time." She prayed for me, and she began to speak in my life concerning my husband. She said, "I hear God saying your husband is coming back, and he going to face some rafter, and you are not going to be able to do anything about. He is not going to get away with the things he has done. Wherever he is at, it is not working out the way he thought it would be or expected to be. I know you're hurting and full of pain, but if you want to know what is going on with your husband, you must use wisdom by not yelling or being aggressive."

She shared her situation about how her husband cheating in their marriage. She said she was very hurt, and it took her a while to forgive, but God had to help in the matter and save their marriage. She said, "I know how you feel and even through the other situation on top of that you had to face. I will keep you in my prayers, and if you need to talk anytime, call me. I love you and stay encouraged, sis."

As time went on, I began to feel myself coming together. I never slept in my bedroom. I slept on the floor in the second bedroom where my mother was sleeping at that time. The only time I would go in my bedroom was to pray in the closet, use my bathroom, and get dressed. I have been going to church and out on different occasions to restaurants and functions. I got busy with school and family. On December 10, 2017, my husband texted me on Messenger:

"Do not have a phone yet, so I can't call you. I just remember about Messenger, but I must wait when I am around WiFi. Did you go to the doctor?"

I never responded back. I felt like if he was not able to come with me to the doctor, why ask me if I went. He left me to face that situation alone. He put me there in the first place.

I took my mother to purchase a new cellphone. As the salesperson was assisting her, I received a phone call from my sister-in-law. She was trying to reach her brother to let him know that his mother had to have an emergency surgery. I told her to call him on Messenger.

She called again to talk and update me own her mother's status. She was trying to still contact her brother as well to inform him about their mother's situation. I told her she can contact him through Messenger or video call him on Facebook. But she said she no longer has Messenger (Facebook). I told her I would reach out to him and tell him to call you regarding his mother. I really did not want to go that way, but for my mother-in-law, I proceeded on.

On January 03, 2018, at 9:42 a.m. on Messenger I sent this "Merry Christmas/Happy New Year's and Happy Birthday." At 1:48, he responded, "Oh, you remember I exist. I thought you forgot about me. I do not have a phone. I can only use Messenger sometimes. Well, Merry Christmas and Happy New Year to you too. I miss you and I love you." On January 03, 2018 at 2:23 p.m., he sent this: "Want to come home, but I know you hate me right now. Not trying to come there to fight and argue." He sent "This is for you" at 2:56 p.m. It was a video of a young man talking about financial blessings, and he said he had to send it to twenty-one people to receive financial blessings why not you.

I read, but I did not respond back until January 03, 2018 at 5:41 p.m. "We need to talk most definitely. You need to call your sister. It is about your mother. She called me to talk and update me on your mother's status." He had a little attitude, maybe because I did not respond back with affection. His respond was, "I do not have a phone. Hello! And I am not around WiFi like that. Enough to use Messenger."

My statement was, "You can call people and video call on Messenger too. I have done it and still do. Anyway, your mother had a major surgery on her head because she fell. It caused an internal bleeding. She has a hole in her head that needed to be closed." His response was, "Okay, thanks for telling me. I appreciate it. How is everything with you though besides the obvious? And you must be around Wi-Fi to do all of that when your phone is off. I am in PA, where WiFi is not available like that. I just happen to be in the city now."

My response was, "It doesn't matter. I have to go. My phone is about to die. I am traveling right now. You can use your friends' phone or whoever you are with to contact your sister. I will let her know I text you about it already."

He responded, "Okay, you still love me?" I responded, "Of course." He responded, "Okay, I love you too. Call me or text me on Messenger when you get a chance, please. And I when or if I can, I will respond. Take care baby (with a heart symbol)."

My husband returned home on January 17, 2018, at 7:42 a.m. He stated how he was living with a friend and his girlfriend. She was complaining about him eating up the kid's food among everything else. He was not comfortable living at his friend's house with his family. He talked about how he had all this money and wasted by partying, going to bars, and staying in hotels. He stated nothing was not working out the way he wanted it to and he was losing more than gaining. He was moving around from different people's house to stay because where he was at originally, he did not want to be there too much. On January 12, 2018, at 1:03 p.m., his response was, "I have an issue, babe. Bed bugs. I am covered with bites. It is nasty where I am at. They are not clean people. If I come, I must strip in the garage and go straight into the shower. I just wanted you to know about the bug situation. I am back in PA at my friend's house. This where I been for most of the part. I'm trying to get a car. Things are not where I expected them to be, going out all the time with friends, spending little money I have on food and drinks. I'm just lost right now, trying to find my way, and I need help, and I have no one to call on. I will find my eventually because I have faith."

As my husband was sharing this with me, I thought about when I asked him to send me a hundred dollar to restore the light. He said, "I let you know if I have it or not. If I have some money to contribute, I will let you know." Then when he tells me about how he messed up all the money he had going out with his friends at hotel, bars, and drinks whatever else. I could not believe he was saying this when I asked him to send me a hundred dollars to cut back on the lights. Wow!

God, I am sorry and tired of this marriage and feeling like I am unimportant. I feel lonely, and I am really hurting inside my heart, mind, and body. I do not deserve to be treated like I am a nobody. I feel like escaping into another world where I can really know how it truly feels to be loved like a queen. All I ever got through or out of relationships was what they can get or gain from their own well-being. I only received loved when its freshly in the beginning of a relationship. I just want to know how it feels to really be loved and continued to flow in that same capacity of love throughout life. I'm tired of that type of love where they love you for a moment and then decides they want to treat you by lying, being deceitful, dishonest, sneaky, conning, fornication, saying hurtful words, cursing words, and being used. Love is genuine. It shows realness of effects. Love does speak with honesty of admitting to your wrongdoing, but you learned from your situations. Also it does not return or even continue in wrongdoing. The love of God will make you want to make things right between both, who is right and wrong. It is about listening, having respect, and being patient with understanding of the needs of both parties. Having the love of Christ does work well in any relationship (marriage, family, children, or friends) because you will find happiness, forgiveness, honesty, joy, peace, respect, and a caring heart to be open to any circumstances that you or someone else might face. True love is the answer to all your problems, circumstances, or obstacles in life. If you are ready to submit, humble oneself, and commit to whatever you face in life through good or hardship, you can make it with the right love, understanding, and patience.

I was told twice that I need to stop living in a fantasy world like Cinderella and the prince. This is how life is. People go through relationships and arguments and making mistakes. There no such thing as a happy life in this world. If you keep thinking it, you are going to be all alone and you'll grow old and miserable. Wow! I still never had the real opportunity to see what I truly long for in my heart. I truly wonder could it really be true will I ever be loved and treated like a Cinderella or the queen. However, I believe my time will come exactly when it is that appointed time to receive that true love that will bring peace and happiness to my soul. It is okay to hold on to faith and hope because anything is possible when you have Jesus. I must stay on my focus point, which is the love of God.

After my husband came back home, I told him everything was

taken care of because of God sought my needs. The lawsuit came through from my dad, which he left me and my sister assets before he died. I encouraged my husband to go back to school and focus on getting his degree. I said, "We are fine financially because of God. He said he will never leave me, nor will he forsake me. He will supply all my needs no matter what circumstance may fall upon my life." My husband said that he will put in for unemployment to help as well toward the household.

I took care of all the bills, pay my tithes, took care of my sons and my mom, brought me a brand-new beautiful vehicle, clothes, and took care of my vision where the enemy tried to snatch it away. I also gave my husband money and brought clothes, which I did not want to because I was still hurt and in pain. I still went out to dinner and movies, which was my treat. My husband did not still have to worry about anything because his beautiful, good-hearted wife forgave him and continued to show him love. I still was cautious about things, so I took complete control over the household. I was not falling back into the same situation (state) that I came out of from—my husband's lying, cheating, cruelty, hatred, selfishness of not paying the bills, and keeping the money for himself, and then bailing out on his family.

My husband tried to be intimate, and I said, "I do not think so. We're not having sex at all until you get yourself tested. We are going to my doctor where I can know everything is accurate." He said, "I got tested already. I seen a truck on the street that had a sign where you can get tested." I said, "That is good, but I need to know for my own safety because I do not believe nothing you're saying anyway." He tried to give me attitude, and I said, "This is my body. Either you do or not, I do not really care. This is my life, not yours, and I have to look out for me for now on."

The next day, my husband said, "Whatever you want to do, I will go with you to get tested." We were debating first on where to go because he did not have any health insurance. We were going to go to a free clinic, but he was saying he did not feel comfortable of going to those types of clinics. He said he'd rather go to my doctor where he feels comfortable. My husband was tested on February 1, 2018, for everything. I called the doctor a week ago to find out about the results, but my husband had to give authorization, which did not make any sense because I was the wife. The following day (February 15, 2018), I called again because my husband said I should put him on the phone to give the okay. The reception indicated again, and my husband was on a two-way and said, "Yes, that is my wife. It's fine." The receptionist got his file and said, "Everything was good, but he had a trait of sickle cells." He said that his father had the disease or trait, and it was passed down to his kids.

In a week, I was not feeling comfortable not yet. Then I was talking to God who put reassurance in my heart. I allowed my husband to be intimate with me at that time. I still felt hurt because my mind kept thinking about who he was with and what I was put through. My husband was home all the time and going to school as well. I was beginning to feel a little difference in our marriage. I was still praying and seeking God.

My husband fell back into doing the same thing. He was supposed to come home after class. I texted him at 9:24 p.m. and asked him why he was not answering his phone. He said, "I'm coming, babe, just went to the bar for a minute with my peoples. Be back by twelve." The text was sent at 11:02 p.m. on February 22, 2018. It seems the more you pray, the harder the enemy tries to work against you, but God my creator still remains in my will continually because he felt my pain and heard my cries. He continually to came to my rescue because I decided a long time ago to stay in my Father's will, praying, fasting, and reading his Word. I have built a closer relationship with my Father whom I cannot live without. He is my everything. God gave me several scriptures to comfort me through my journey of facing obstacles (Psalms 23, Psalms 91, Matthew 6:9–13). He also put people in my life that was able to pray me through and encourage me as well. These people were my mother, belated father, belated brother, sister, two best friends, belated Darnette Dickey (deceased), and Lakiesha Davis (present), prophetess and prophetic, unknown people who just came up to me to give encouragements, godmother, pastors, and ministers. My God is an awesome God because when you seem to be close to giving up and you reach a point where you're not able to handle your task, God comes at the right time, which is the truth because his Word said he will never, never ever leave you or forsake you. God will not abandon his people in times of need unless you avoid him or turn your back on him.

Listen, I almost lost my mind to a point where my house was being violated by my husband's infidelity. My own husband was having sex in my house with the neighbors. One was a married Caucasian woman, another was a young African American young lady the same age as my baby boy who was dating the young lady, other young girls who works at ShopRite, and more. My husband was utilizing my garage for his own personal pleasures and in my rooms. I see things that was shown to me to let me know he had them in my home, such as the sheets and the pillows were used, a smell of perfume. My husband had the smell of sex on him. Doors were opened in my house that I know I had closed. I would set up a trap just to see who it was, such as putting things behind the doors to see if someone goes in, and I would know because the objects were being moved. I remember going to church with my sister and her husband. When I came home, I was led to the closet door downstairs. I went to grab my husband's book bag and opened it up. There were condoms in his bag, and one was used.

His statement was clear. They were giving out condoms at his job where he works at, an auto parts store warehouse really.

Listen, everyone, I almost lost my mind. but God did not permit it to happen. I would cry all the time. He did not want me to use his phone or even give me the password. He would distance himself, never did anything with me, but go food-shopping and watch movies on television. He never took the initiative to buy me dinner when he is out or clothes on his own.

I could not think, breathe, or concentrate right because my mind was thinking of all the things that he's done to me and wondering what my husband was doing. If something didn't seem right or if it was different, I would wonder why he did that or he never did this before or what's taking him so long or why he doesn't want to get pick up. I could not even go to my internship without wondering who was at my house or why he was getting off early or why he did not answer his phone. I would watch him like a hawk. The enemy caused a great distraction that almost took my mind. I was operating like a dysfunctional person; my mind was almost completely gone. It was very unhealthy for me to live this way. I was not paying attention to my life and myself. I needed some attention and staying focused. I needed to care about me, love me, smile again, be happy, go shopping, get my hair done, go out with my girlfriends, and live again. I needed to trust me for me by allowing myself to take a leap of faith and live again. I needed to gain my heart back that was put in the wrong hands. He did not know how to take care it, so I needed to take it back and give it to God completely as a whole again. My husband was not ready for this special, warm-hearted person; he did not know how to embrace her and take care of her. God gave my husband a saved, faithful, warm-hearted, special human being, and he took advantage of a person who has a beautiful heart and soul. He was not ready for my warm, special heart, so now I decided to hold on to it in a box until I see signs that indicate he's worthy to have it back. I would still treat him with kindness and love, but my heart will be under a safety net with God. God has complete control over my warm, special heart.

I used to say to myself, how can you trust a man or woman who puts you through hurt and pain? It is easy to say I trust you when you are not the one whose heart was hurt. You're at ease, you're good, you are not wondering or thinking crazy thoughts or up late crying and cannot sleep. You are with smiles and laughter and talking about you do not have a problem with trust. You do not have trust issues. You do not have to look over your shoulder and play detective. You do not have to suspect everyone's motives. I know how to behave myself around friends, new people, family member, coworkers, or males without lusting after them. You stand with a free mind and spirit. Your shoes are a safety net with no worries or regret.

They think that they are in a safety net, but in reality, their world will crumble down. They may pretend that they hold no worries or regret, but it hits their conscience at some point. They begin to wonder and form a straight face because they tried to keep the explosion from coming out, but where there is darkness, light will come. It will never stay hidden onto thee (Luke 12:2). We can only be hypocrites or imposters before men, never God. He sees through the actor's mask. Sooner or later, it all shall be revealed.

They do carry holes of a wear and tear because of the behavior pattern they do unto people. However, as a warranty contract from God manufactured in heaven, which usually stipulate that damage from wear and tear (corroded) will not be covered under sin. You can give your life to God by the forgiveness of sin and restoring back the wear and tear that you have created because of the damage you made to people's lives. In the Bible, God tell us to repent of our sins of the things that we have hidden in our hearts and actions.

The person whose heart was hurt takes a great healing to mend that hurt and pain.

Chapter 12

MAKING JUDGMENT CALLS ON OTHERS WILL ALWAYS TURN INTO A JUDGMENT CALL UNTO YOU

Note: Please do not never think or say it could not be me because you never know what can happen soon as you turn that corner. You be saying never could well be me this day and now it's happening to me the next day. I never could have imagined this would happen to me in my lifetime. You never know when you're faced with that same or other issues and how you're going to react. We all are human beings who take in pain and handle the situations differently but still need support, love, and guidance.

However, I stayed in contact with pastors, prophetess, and praying lines. I listened to gospel music, read the Bible and prayed with my mother. This was what kept my mind from being under attack by the devil's tasks (the destructive devil). I always say to let this mind be the mind of Christ at all times. I had to stay focused on God and do the work of God. This was what kept me stay alive and well. I had to let God continue to fight my battles and dealing with my husband. I could not stand in God's way because he gave orders to let him handle it, and I just stayed humble, focused, and I continued to serve God. God told me when you step into the matter, you cause disaster because you sometimes let fresh come in or you just do not know when to fall back. God said this was his task of dealing with my husband. He also said, "You just continue to be a faithful humble wife even when you get cursed at, lied on, get mistreated, abused verbally and physically (throwing objects in my face, putting his hands on my neck, and punching me on the right side of my eye twice). I took legal action toward my husband. I reported his behavior while at the emergency room and another time at my residence. August 4, 2020, was the day I pressed charges against my husband for domestic violence. He was place on a forty-eight-hour hold for domestic violence at the Wallace Police Department. He was released and assigned a court date on September 23, 2020, at 9:30 a.m. to meet the judge for assault. My husband was ordered to pay a fine of $250 and a year of probation, and if he violates his probation of any charges, he has to do a full turn of a year in jail.

Note: I was so angry when my husband assaulted me in my face. I just stood there screaming with my fist balled up. I wanted to strike back, but I looked down at my granddaughter who was crying out loud and pulled myself together. This was because she needed me, and I could not allow myself to get arrested as well. I handled it the right way and let the authority of the police department handle this situation. The hurt part about it was when my husband laughed in my face, while trying to apologize when he was released from jail. I said, "Why are you laughing like it's a joke? This is not funny at all. What you feel inside it's going to come out as the truth." I told him he needs to go to his sister's house because you're not taking this marriage seriously. He looked sad and pretended he was packing his clothes. I went by my business and paid him no mind. When I went out the door to go to the office, he started panicking and saying, "You're not going to call the police on me again." My response was, "I'm going to take care some business at the office." This was my choice in the protection for myself.

I was not afraid to speak out because my body was special to me. I am not a punching bag for no one. I will not tolerate physical abuse. I definitely did not deserve this type of reaction of violence toward me. You must fight back and let it be known to the authorities. Sometimes people need a wake-up call, Christians or non-Christians. I love you enough to report your behavior, and I mean business. My husband was apologizing and saying, "I did not mean to hit you. I just mush you." I said, "Whether you mush or hit, they both are wrong. You're not supposed to have any contact of verbal and physical abuse toward anybody. My space is my space, and you are not supposed cross that line. I am a woman and not a dude. I love my face and body. I know God got my back, and the authorities that he put in charge on this earth does as well."

I never experienced physical abuse before with my husband until now. It was crazy because I would not back down by using my voice, and I told God I refused to be in an abusive relationship. I would not be a victim of an abuser. My husband never did this as long as we've been together. I see pure evil formed from my husband's eyes. The devil even spoke out and said, "You're not a Christian. You think that oil you put around this house is going to do anything. You're wicked and evil. I hate you, and I can't stand you, you bitch, you dog, you evil person. You're lazy. You don't clean or cook. I know other females who act better than you and are dying to be with me. Females who are willing to suck my dick. You're not a wife because you don't do nothing for me at all. I hate you and can't stand to look at you. You're insecure, and I had to get stuck with you. You're too jealous, you bum. You got all the college degrees and still not working. You need to get a job. Nobody wants you, and you're going to grow old by yourself."

God told me, "You're fighting with spirits, and it is using your husband's body. Do not look at your husband, but look at the enemy that is using him. My husband had a raging spirit along with a lust, deceit, lies, jealousy, cheating, smoking, alcohol, foul mouth, and selfish spirit."

A longtime spiritual dear friend gave me this book called Prayers that Rout Demons: Prayers for Defeating Demons and Overthrowing the Power of Darkness. I truly forgot she gave me this book. It was kept down in my garage inside a tote or hamper. God drew me right to the book when I was going down to the garage to see what my husband was up too. I went to my hamper looking through it when I came across this book. God told me to read certain passages out loud in my home.

1. Warfare Prayer
2. Prayer to Root out
3. Release the Power of the Blood
4. Prayers for Divine Safety and Protection

5. Deliverance from Serpents
6. Prayer Against Jezebel
7. Deliverance and Renunciation of Sexual Sin

    I told my mother about how God led me to this book; I was going for one thing and ended up retrieving this book. I said, "A spiritual friend gave me this book a very long time ago." My mother said, "Sometimes God will bring it back to you when he knows you are ready for it at that particular time or moment. Apostle Glover always says that God gives us books, but we do not read it at that time, or it is not that time for us to read them at that moment. Sometimes the book is meant to have for a reason at another time frame. God will store up things and bring it back at that particular time when it is needed to help us in a time of need.

    I began to utilize the book while my mother was on the phone, as well as continuing on my own throughout my home. I would do spiritual cleaning with ammonia mixed with water and holy anointed oil. I would put Holy anointed oil on my doors, windows, closets inside and out, bathrooms and front door, and downstairs garage, which was my greater task throughout my home as I prayed. I was determined to fight against every unclean spirit that dwell in my home. It had to leave my home in the name of Jesus. I would see spirits in my home, and I would say, "The blood of Jesus and the devil is a liar." This took place at my townhome in New Jersey of 2018.

    I remember God had me to go down to the garage, which was my heavy battle. The unclean spirits were very heavy, and they were in the garage. I took my ammonia, water, and holy oil mixed in a spray bottle along with a bottle of holy oil to anoint the area. I threw out a mattress I took down; they are from one of the bedrooms with other belongings a while ago. God told me to throw it out; it had been used but it was still good. I threw out other items as well and put it outside from the garage to be thrown into the dumpster (a spiritual cleaning). My husband came home and seemed to be very upset. He stated, "Why did you throw out the mattress? It's going to rain." However, there were other things thrown out for trash as well, but he kept focusing on the mattress for some reason. I said, "Why is it your concern if it's going to rain or not? It is going into the dumpster for garbage. That is the only thing you see—the mattress. There are other items as well." I got very angry and said, "Why you so focused on that mattress? Is it because I disturbed your comfort zone? God sees and knows everything, especially when you are doing unclean things." He did not say anything else after I said what I said. I remember the married neighbor across from me was standing outside in front of her garage. She started to watch me remove things from my garage. She then got in her car as if she were about to drive off, but she continued to watch me the whole time. This was one of the females my husband had been involved with. I would see her wave secretly and smile at my husband, and I have seen her at my husband's job one day. I was parked across my husband's job when I saw her coming from the other side driving off quickly. I have confronted my husband on several occasions about the neighbor and others. I remember when I found a condom in my husband's book bag, and one was missing because condoms come in a pack of three. I confronted my husband about it, and he said his job was passing out condoms, so he just took it and put it in his book bag.

Listen, world, why would an auto part store pass out condoms when they deal with car parts. My husband was working at an auto part store warehouse. I told my husband, "Why would you accept something we do not use? You did not think to call or tell me about it." He gets mad at me when I am saying something that is true and right. An agitated person reveals itself when you speak the truth. They will try to turn the table on you as if you are the one who is crazy. The blood of Jesus.

You may say to yourself she is crazy to still be involved in all this mess that her husband put her through, or it couldn't be me because I wouldn't have tolerated it, or what's wrong with her, she must be mind-controlled or settled or blinded. I have a complete healthy mind and plenty of time if I was going to bail out. However, God spoke to me, and others have a prophecy to me concerning my marriage. God said to stand still and be unremovable. He said, "The battle is not yours. It belongs to me. Stay focused on me and not your man." God said that he will deal with my husband, and he would have no choice to submit himself to me and repent of his wrongdoing. God said we all must pay a price when we do wrong to others, that people make judgment upon their self. We are not to judge but pray for them. God said he makes the judgment, and he deals with the person in his own way.

God said, "You continue to go before me in prayer, fasting and reading your Bible." God also said that there are many marriages especially holy people who bail out or quit because of the man or woman done hurt them bad. They never learned to forgive, and they never reconciled the situation among each other.

God said, "When you went to the altar and commit yourself to one another in saying those vows 'I take you to be my wife [or husband], to have and to hold from this day forward for better, for worse, for richer or for poor in sickness and in health, to love and cherish, 'til death do us apart, according to God's holy law, and this is my solemn vow.'" Listen, when it was said "for better or for worse," God didn't set a limited on what better or worse was supposed to look like. Your worse is your worse. It has no limits. It can be drawn to anything in your life. God did not set any laws on what your worse and better days should be because everyone faces a different storm in their marriage. You are going to have your ups and downs; you may even be dealing with your loved one's past issues. That is why vows are important when you repeat it to each other because you made a commitment to honor that which was said to each other. However, we must admit to ourselves that we knew what we walk into when we dedicate our life to that special one. The choice was ours, not God especially when we act quickly to move in without an approval.

God just puts it plain and simple because our life can be faced with many of obstacles that may come our way, whether it's good or bad news, poor or rich, sickness and health that we should love and cherish it all. He did not draw a map or picture of it of how the scenery should be modeled as. The worse, better, or anything else holds no limits, except for if that man or woman commit unclean acts of sexual immorality etc. This violates the commitment in marriage between the husband and wife, who supposed to be dedicated (faithful, trustworthy, and respect) toward each other as partners.

The only thing that God says in the Bible about marriage/divorce that can be a very difficult matter if that man or woman commits adultery, sexual immorality, marries another, and marries her who is divorced commits adultery (Mathew 19:3–9). God will judge. God does give permission through the body of his law (ground rules), for that man or woman to file for divorce due to adultery, sexual immorality in a marriage. However, God is not demanding or ordering it to take place or a mandatory, but he does give authority or consent for it to happen among the spouses. When there is no sincere regret, remorse, or reconciliation, that have not been occurred. God does want the spouses to work out their difference in any situation whether its other marital problems or adultery. God would rather for you to get it right to work out those obstacles that became a problem in your marriage. He wants every marriage to work because he does honor marriage.

A century ago, in the Old Testament, they were stoned to death if such thing as adultery or sexual immorality were to take place in a marriage. During the period, a couple that was said to be betrothed, which means engaged to be married, marriage proposal, or simply engaged, they were also stoned to death if such fornication or unfaithfulness was taking place during the betrothal period. In the biblical times, they took engagement as the same as being married. In the Old Testament, they carried the death penalty, and in the New Testament, they carried the option of "putting away" (Releation.co). There were no ties or bonds together among the spouses. They were free to move on in life without holding any ties together. However, the law has change from century ago. The natural law states they are to get a divorce if such adultery was committed between either of the spouses while they are joined in marriage.

Which would you rather be, stoned to death, put away, or work out your difference in your marriage? We are to thank God that they did not kept that law of being stoned to death or put away to free yourself from a cheating spouse (adultery). In all reality, I'd rather be a bride (wife) who is sanctified, loyal to my groom (husband) to avoid being stone to death or be put away. This was due to having a fiancé or a bond contract that was vowels or commitment of engagement to be broken. In the biblical times, everything that was wrongfully happening to their eyes was punished by taking someone's life to solve the problems. The sad thing about this was that at some point in time, they were wrongfully accused.

In the biblical times, Joseph and Mary gives a living example of betrothal. Joseph was betrothed to Mary. They had an arranged agreement or a sealed contract with each other.

During the time of their engagement, Joseph has learned of Mary's pregnancy, which he grew puzzled in his mind. He did not understand Mary being with child, being that they were engaged to be married. At that time, Joseph did not know of the blessing or miracle that Mary was conceiving a child through the Holy Spirit. This most definitely seemed to be awkward or strange to Joseph. He thought in his mind that Mary committed an act of fornication or just violated their arrangement of marriage (betrothal). Joseph was a righteous man, and he had in his plan to set up an arrangement to divorce or put Mary away for such behavior that was conducted quietly. Joseph did not want to put Mary to shame by exposing her to the public (Matthew 1:18–19). Joseph did learn that Mary, the mother of Jesus Christ, was conceived through the Holy Spirit before they came together.

However, if Mary were found to be having fornication or sexual intimate to other than her fiancé Joseph while in an arranged or bond contract, she would have been found guilty of committing adultery. There would not been any mention of Mary conceiving Jesus, the son of God because she would have been stoned to death or put away. The unrevealing shadow walker was working his schemes back in the biblical time as well.

Marriage is very honorable in the eyesight of God. However, before you take such commitments until marriage, think before you say "I do" or committing sin in the marriage. God did set the law down of committing such sin of adultery and sexual immorality in the marriage. God does prefer for that husband and wife to mend things in having a forgiving heart. Joseph's eyes were blinded, and his ears were closed. All he saw and heard at that time was Mary was pregnant. How was that possible when they were in a binding contract? He let his emotions and feelings almost get the best of him, letting Mary go on her own (divorce). God came on in the scenery and spoke to his son Joseph on how Mary had conceived a child. Joseph allowed his eyes to be opened and receive what has been taking place in his contract. This made his spirit at ease with the situation of knowing the truth. Joseph accepted what the will of the Father, which was a spirit planted a seed inside the womb of Mary. Joseph married Mary and took on the role of Jesus's natural father to raise according to God.

God did not say marriage was not supposed to be easy, but we must forgive when the hurtfulness, disappointment, and pain come at us. I was at my better days, and then I hit my worse (betrayal, lying, adultery, jealousy, and abuse). It tried to come up against my health and make me sick (adultery and being tested from my husband's infidelity). It tried to destroy my integrity and drain me dry, but God still provided. My husband tried to destroy me by not taking care of his responsibility as a husband in the household. We did not have any food, hot water was off, almost being evicted from not paying the rent, and we had no cooking gas. God opened the door for my inheritance to come through, and my mother and oldest son were there for me financially and spiritually. God would not allow me to fall because I belong to him, and he is my savior through the time of the storm.

I do not have to act the way others have treated and hurt me because I truly want to make it to heaven, and I don't want to disappoint God by doing evil for evil. This is a hard task, but God will not give us anything that we cannot handle or unable to survive through these obstacles that are faced in our life.

To the men and women, I need you to understand that God loves you all. He does not want you to drift off into a deep sleep by being mesmerized by your own fantasy world. God does not want you to stay in another dimension or a make-believe island. He needs you to zoom back out into reality and face what is true in front of you. We cannot think that the things we want in accepting the wrong desires, needs, and wants will be acceptable to God. It will not be in the righteousness of God's will in his eyesight. Therefore, we must uncover our eyes to see what God has in need for that individual to fit our own special needs. So let the covers fall off to see what is behind the scenery. Because as long as you detain it, how can God detach it? 1 Peter 4:2 (KJV) says, "That he no longer should live the rest of his time in the flesh to lusts of men, but to the will of God." 1 Peter 4:2 (NLT) states, "You won't spend the rest of your lives chasing your own desires, but you will be anxious to do the will of God."

However, men and ladies, be careful who you allow or accept into your bedroom. You need to take the blindfold off to see what is really between your sheets. Take control in the will of God and uncover your bedsheets or throw back the bedsheets to see what is in between your sheets (a wolf in sheep's clothing, the unrevealing shadow walker).

    1. Is it John with the anger/rage problems?
    2. Is it Billy with the selfish ways?
    3. Is it Anthony with the lying tongue?
    4. Is it Nancy the prostitute?
    5. Is it Corey, the male prostitute?

6. Is it Sally, the deceitful?
7. Is it Bobby with the gambling problem?
8. Is it Kim with the attitude and the one who betrays?
9. Is it Katrina, the drug addict?
10. Is it Ralph, the alcoholic?
11. Is it James with the tight pocket (stingy)?
12. Is it Mary, who does not make commitments?
13. Is it Rafael, who does not make commitments?
14. Is it Luis with no responsibility or does not accept responsibilities?
15. Is it Blue or Ivory who is just saying no to everything if it does not involve them?
16. Is it Joe the jobless or unemployed person?
17. Is it Jason with the thug life mentality by the name of psycho or maniac?
18. Is it Henry with the violent and raging spirit?
19. Is it Kathy with the stealing problem?
20. Is it Christ the gay or bisexual?
21. Is it Monica the lesbian?
22. Is it Adam with STD?
23. Is it Lukas the rapper?
24. Is it Fahima or Joseph the molesters?
25. Is it Ashley or Ben with the mental behavior problems?
26. Is it Alex with HIV or AIDS?

Surprise, men and women. That's right, you can be so eager or determined to subject yourself to the wrong company because you desire what your flesh seeks or go after by working or operating into lust. You do not even know what he or she is bringing in between your bedsheets up above (1-26). The shadow walkers do not give warnings, only destructions. So, men and women of God, keep your bedsheets ivory or clean and spick and span until God sends what he has for your needs. Be so careful not to throw back your sheets for the wrong reasons. Like Juanita Bynum said, no more sheets, no more allowing Rick, Harry, Jonathan, Kelly, or Martha in between your sheets because the queen sizes, king sizes, full sizes, or twin sizes are befouled without marriage.

I can contest to this because I contracted the wrong company in between my white linen sheets—the lying spirit, adultery spirits, raging and violent spirits, male Jezebel spirit, disease spirit (AIDS), which tried to kill me or bring harm to me, but God did not permit them to take place through my youngest son's father (it didn't succeed because I did not give my body away), the user, alcoholic, drugs and smoking spirit, living a double life spirit or jealousy and deceitful spirit, etc.

I have asked myself how can I read this life story about my life or tell it because it brings back hurt and pain and tears to my eyes just by reading my story. Then I realized as I look back over the years of my life, I could have been dead and gone. God sought purpose for my life even through my storm. I am glad to be alive and well, but most importantly, I made it over by God's grace and mercy. The devil thought he made have defeated me or won, but I proved to him he has lost the battle. I have utilized my fight in the battle by crying out, praying, consulting God in my praying closet, reading, and fasting to defeat the enemy.

God spoke and said people need to hear what I have been through and still going through. But the process is being formed in healing every wound. They need to know they are not alone, and they can call on God and stay in the will of God to overcome any obstacles in their marriage or in their life. God is still working on my marriage. We are not where we used to be because God's grace and mercy, through the prayers of a strong, faithful righteous woman of God (wife) and the prayer warriors, is showing manifestation. Everything is a process in God's timing, not man. "For what God has for you, it is for you. Trust his timing. Trust his plan."

God gave me instructions concerning my marriage. I was told to dedicate our wedding rings back up to heaven for seven days. I would get up every day and take my husband's and my rings while he was asleep with the holy oil and dedicated them back to God. I would pour some oil inside my hands and take the rings and soak them into the holy oil and lift my hands with both rings up to heaven.

I would pray these words:

God, I dedicate these rings back to you under your wings of

heaven. God, this marriage belongs to you; it is no longer in my hands. I pray that you will ordain this marriage to be holy and righteousness before your throne. God, if any unclean spirit that laid upon this marriage, please remove it. I pray against every male or female Jezebel spirit, lying tongue, adultery, separation, divorce, fornication, jealousy, hatred, alcoholic, smoking, foul mouth spirits, rage, violent spirits, anger, lust, stingy, disrespectful spirit, lack of communication, sneakiness, bitterness, hurt, and pain. I pray against every stronghold. Please take it away in Jesus's holy name and keep it sanctified under your holy blood. God, I pray that my husband and I will have great communication, laughter, joy, love, loving on each other, understanding, forgiveness, taking time out for each other, listening to each other concerns, allowing him to only have eyes for me as I do for him, respecting one another and being mindful toward each other's feelings. I pray that we will lead by example of your holy word of what you ordained marriage to be. We will be a living example among other married people. I pray that this marriage will last a lifetime until you take us home to your kingdom. We shall live and not die.

I pray in Jesus's name that you shall guide us and lead us in the way that we shall go and not our own way. I pray in Jesus's name that our minds shall always be the mind of Christ. We shall worship you together, pray, and fast together as a husband and wife in Jesus's name. I pray in Jesus's name that no weapon shall be formed up against our marriage shall not prosper in Jesus's holy name.

I pray that you will bring our family together in unity, my oldest and youngest son and stepdaughter in love and peace. I pray in Jesus's name that they will have forgiveness in their hearts and leave the past where it shall be. God, I ask you in your holy name to let my family come with an open heart of joy, laughter and cherish those moments of family gatherings and holidays that we can have together along with our grandchildren. I pray in Jesus's name, a new beginning chapter of a greater love that will fall upon our family.

God, I thank you for my marriage, children, and grandchildren that you have formed together in being a part of our marriage together as a whole family. God, I speak those things as if they were, and I end this prayer with two scriptures: "Our father which are in heaven" (Matthews 6:9) and "The Lord is my shepherd" (Psalms 23). Amen.

P.S. I also take the holy oil and anoint my husband's shoes every morning, saying cover him with your blood as he goes out, guide his footsteps, and do not let him stray away in his own path. God, guide his mind and thoughts to be of purity and holiness. God, let him leave out and come back as a faithful and righteous husband. God, he is in your hands because I gave him back to you. Amen.

God gave me seven days to quote this prayer, but I continue to say it every day.

I decided to focus completely on God as he handles my marriage and family. I gave God that battle to fight and stood still as he told me to do so. Every battle was not for me to fight; I just pray and leave it in the hands of God. God chooses what battle we must fight in and what battle he fights to complete the task. In the battle, he may just need us to do certain things just pray, fast, and read his holy word, or minister or speak into the life of people at that moment. We are to speak the word of God but not force people to be changed or turn their life around. No, that God's job—to take over and make a change in an individual's life. He knows just what it takes to grab hold of that person's attention to make a change in their life.

We need to stay in our lanes and do not cross over to God's lane. This is how we face bad traffic when we cross over to God's lane. We run the red light (don't stop or yield to the Holy Spirit), speed (don't slow down and take heed to what God is saying to us), don't yield to signs (don't submit or humble ourselves), go over to other people's lanes (get involved or mixed up into other people's affair instead of tending to our own affairs), do U-turns on certain streets (instead of letting God guide your way, you turn and go the opposite way that leads into trouble), go down a one-way street and cutting people off (overpowering people just to get by or ahead of someone to have your way), or don't have the patience to wait when the traffic gets heavy (you get impatient by rushing to handle things your own way instead of letting God move on your behalf). We tend to go over to the side of the road to try and get through traffic (slide swap or cause damage, you make your own lane just to fit your own needs). We also become distracted by diverting our attention from the road by talking to the cell phone, sending text messages, or eating food, instead of focusing on the road (we gossip our attention on unnecessary conversations, rumors, or among other things and not focusing on God). This is how we allow our eyes to be blinded through distractions because we feel no threat or have no conscience in our doing wrong or being mindful. Then before we know it, we just cause a bad accident to occur because we were not patient enough to wait on God and not being mindful of the things we do or attempt to do. We tend to do things when we want to or how we want to. We make our own judgment calls on the matter and how to hurry up the process. However, when we cross God's lane, we cause our own disasters or dilemma to occur because we could not wait or stay in our own lanes. God does not need you to do his job by taking over the steering wheel completely. God controls how things should be in our life. God set the boundaries of setting certain limits in a respectable manner.

Listen, when you push your way through bad traffic by going past the rules and regulations, you cause your own circumstances or obstacles to happen. The consequence does follow when you go above the law in the natural world and the spiritual realm. You just could not be patient or humble yourself to (sustain) submit to God's instructions. You just demonstrated being selfish, and God is not a selfish person. He warns us and shows us things before it happens or takes place in our life.

This is how you slowed up your own healing, deliverance, or blessing to occur. God must take his time now and find another way or solution through bad traffic to fix what you messed up. You have just slowed down your own healing or blessing for another month, days, weeks, or years. The process must start all over again. This does not mean God gave up on you. He sometimes must bring discipline or order to correct disobeying his will. God keeps it stored up in a safety net until he feels you are ready to handle a simple task. I learned that obedience is always the key to gain what you need in life by God. I keep a date night with God always in the morning (7:00 a.m.) and after midnight. God wakes me up at 5:00 or 6:00 a.m. I have the best date night with my Father.

If it were up to the man at the age of one and a half, my life would have been cut short on this earth, but God had other plans for my life.

My mother told me the story of how I got burned when I was a toddler at the age of one and a half years old. I was burned on the left side of my body, such as my ear, cheek, arm, leg, and had a skin graft on both of my thighs. I was announced dead. My brother was two and a half years old, and my little sister was six months old.

How it all began was about 3:00 a.m. one day. A two-storage building was left unattended by the landlord and had caught on fire, which led to uncontrollable blazing flames.

My mother and my dad were living in a one-bedroom apartment on Eighteenth Avenue and moved to a two-bedroom apartment building on 239 South Tenth Street on the third floor in Newark, New Jersey, to provide more space for the family. They also lived in the apartment building with other relatives such as my grandmother Catherine, Uncle Ralph, and one granddaughter who took care of the first floor. When my grandmother Catherine died, her other children took over her apartment—Uncle Jack, Aunt Carolina, and Aunt Annie and their children. My parents have also moved in after my grandmother died on the third floor.

My mother said she and my father were sleeping in bed as her children. My baby sister was sleeping in her crib, which was in my parents' room by the wall. My parents' bedroom was near the living room, and my oldest brother and I were in the room together, sleeping on a bunkbed near the kitchen area. There were only two ways out, through the front door and through the kitchen on the side (back of the building). My parents' first entrance was from the front door of the building up to the third floor. Once you get to the third floor into the hallway, there were two ways to enter their apartment (two doors to the front). The first door leads to the kitchen, and the second leads to the living room. The kitchen entrance led to a back door, down the stairs, and out into the street. There was not a fire escape or bars to the window to exit the building. The only entrance to exit was the front and back door.

My mother explained she heard her children coughing from the bedroom, which had woken her up. She said she was so drowsy and hot as she got up from the bed and went to cut the light switch on the bulb blew out/flicked out. That's when she saw smoke in the bedroom. My mother said she started screaming, "James, the house is on fire!" My father jumped up from the bed, and he grabbed the baby. My parents both went to go retrieve my brother and me from our bedroom, which had no doors attached to either room.

The fire in the apartment was uncontrollable, and my parents began to panic, trying to escape the fire with their children. However, as the smoke and fire were escalating, my parents could not find two of the children in the fire. My mother was still holding on to my baby sister as she was crying out loud and screaming, "Where is my children?" My mother placed my baby sister on the floor in the living room by the window and began to look for me and my brother. My mother felt my brother, grabbed her leg, and she reached for him. Afterward, she said, "I need to get Cat," and my father said, "You cannot get in there because the fire has already escalated in the bedroom coming toward the living room. My father, at that time, was screaming and saying, "Louise, come on! You got to go! It is too late!" She was then starting to yell and scream and hit the window.

At that time, a nice Caucasian man was driving by in a red car and saw my mom at the window along with the smoke. He stopped the car, got out of the car, looked up at the window, and saw my mother hitting the window. He got back in the car, put it in reverse, and went to notify the fire department on South Tenth Street on Central Avenue. The fireman came and took the ladder to retrieve my father and mother, along with the two children from the window (my brother and baby sister). At that time, my mother was hysterically saying, "My baby! My baby! Someone must get my baby." The chief said, "Go around to the back of the building to see what this lady is saying!"

The firemen went inside the building and found me underneath the bed. One of the firemen came out from the back with me in his arm, which I had on an orange T-shirt with black soot from the smoke and black panties. After returning to the front of the building, he yelled out to the chief, "We found her under the bed. She was unresponsive due to smoke inhalation." And he then rushed me to the ambulance, and my mother got in there with me.

I was unconscious and not breathing. The oxygen mask was not taking effect on me at all. My mother began to pray, cried out loud, and said, "Lord, I will preach your word if you give me back my baby." The paramedics were administering the IV into my arms to try and get circulations flowing. Thereafter, I suddenly began to gasp for my breath, and I came through. My mother said she saw how air went out of my body, and it was the hands of God. I was rushed to the burn unit at Maryland Hospital, which is now called UMDNJ, with third-degree burns (my cheek, ear, both hands, and the pinky fingers are spread wide apart, arm and leg on the left side of my body and skin graft on both of my thighs). They took my mother to another room where they stitched her up from the open wounds from hitting the window.

My mother left the hospital and went back to the apartment building. When she came back, there it was, two ladies who asked her did she lived in that building. The ladies said they wanted to take her home to clean her up and provide things for her needs. My mother never knew who these ladies were who came to her rescue.

My mother called them her angels of prayer warriors. They came to her rescue and sought her needs.

My mother said she informed her mother about her crisis, and the family rushed down from North Carolina and Philadelphia to be there for my mother through her crisis. My mother said my grandmother Catherine panicked to get to her daughter Louise. She said, "Uncle Jonny drove my grandmother to New Jersey. As he was driving, my grandmother put her foot on the gas because my Uncle Johnny was not driving fast enough to get to her daughter and her grandchildren."

My mother also stated that my aunt Celestine and Aunt Mary Elisabeth (an angle in heaven 2018) came to the hospital. They came into the room, and my mother was sitting at the foot of the bed. My mother said I was sitting up on the bed, bandaged up, and I looked at her and said, "Mommy, I'm hungry." Everyone in the room started to laugh and could not believe how I was asking for food already. The nurse went to go get food to curb my hunger. The nurse fed me soft food due to my injury.

I stayed in the hospital for almost a year to gain full recovery from my wounds. My mother said there was a black Christian nurse (elderly lady) who attended to my needs. She said the nurse fell in love with me and talked about how pretty I was. She said the nurse came up to her and asked if she and her husband can take me away on their vacation. My mother said she told my father about the nurse's statement on taking me on their vacation. My father and mother did not agree with it at all. This had my mother kind of scared, but she said the lady was not that type of person. The nurse then went on her vacation, and they had assigned me to another nurse. My mother was still troubled in her mind due to the fact that she did not want to leave the hospital. She said that this never happened to her before, that someone wanted to take her child. She said nobody was not going to take her child from her, and God gave her back to her alive and well. My mother continued to stay overnights until I was released from the hospital. I was named after both of my grandparents, whose names are Catherine Lewis and Catherine Hardy as well.

You cannot stop what God wants alive. Not even the enemy could not hold me back from death or face death. God sent his angels there at our rescue in the burning building, and he did not stop performing miracles, even when the mother cried out toward heaven on behalf of her daughter, who they said was already gone. I am a strong soldier who is still standing tall above all the enemy traps. The unrevealing shadow walker thought he would take my life at an early age and throw other hard tactics in my way, but he was proven wrong. My life serves a purpose in God's kingdom here on earth. I am still breathing and functioning in this great atmosphere at the age of fifty years old. God did it, and he can do it again.

A mother cried out to the Lord, "If you give me back my baby, Lord, I will serve you until I die." She made a promise to her Lord and Savior. She continued to serve God until this day at the age of seventy-one. She holds a title as Apostle Mary Hardy (March 22, 1948).

The enemy is mad because I skipped death. God had a purpose and a plan for my life. I never was supposed to be in this life of experience living again. The enemy wanted to keep my life, but God said, "No, she shall live and not die." I skipped over the devil's assignment of the enemy who tried to take my life. I had a jumpstart back (toward my future) on to God's land on earth. God revived me by putting breath back into my body. God said, "You shall breathe again, daughter."

This is a remarkable story of blessings, miracles, and high favors of my King above heaven's golden gates.

Chapter 13

GOD'S LOVE ENDURES ALL THINGS

Love: The Bible talks and teaches us about love, especially following God's will. Beloved, we must love one another, for love is about or of the creator of our Father above heaven. If you love, then you must know of God, for God is love (1 John 4:7, 8). If you do not love, then you do not know my God. Love suffers long and is kind; love does not envy; love does not parade itself, is not puffed up; does not behave rudely, does not seek its own, is not provoke, thinks no evil; does not rejoice in iniquity, but rejoices in truth; bears all things, believes all things, hopes all things; endures all things. Love will never ever fail (1 Corinthians 13:1–8, 13). I want my love to be greater like my King, the Lord, whom I endure and love. I decided it does not matter how I have been mistreated because my Father, who also been let down, lied on, cursed at, prosecuted, talked about, beat, and nailed to the cross. The son Jesus still stayed in the will of loving his own enemy to a point where he gave up his own life so that we can live here on this earth. If we learn to love in the same glorious capacity, regardless of how we may be hurt or disappointed, we can stand on top. We are bigger and greater than the enemy's schemes and deceitful ways. When we love like Jesus, we have overcome anything that came at us wrongfully. Love conquers all things they may come up against us. Loving can change the very heart of man's ways.

About The Author

Prophetess Catherine Martin is a devoted member of the Crossroads of Holiness Church of God Inc. Ministry. She faithfully followed the ministry under the leadership of Apostle Mary L. Hardy until her passing. Apostle Hardy was a loving, caring, compassionate, and dedicated leader who always put God first and diligently sought to meet the needs of the people.

After Apostle Hardy's passing, Prophetess Martin became a member of Emmanuel Temple Deliverance Tabernacle under the leadership of Pastor Elder Louis Sykes, where she served faithfully for the past 2½ years. She officially submitted her resignation letter on September 20, 2023. It was a pleasure for her to be part of such a great ministry during that time.

Currently, she is under the Watch Care of Apostle Laura Leadbetter of the Newark, New Jersey Ministry. Apostle Leadbetter is not only her spiritual guide but also her godmother and the best friend of her late mother.

Gifted with a strong prophetic calling, Prophetess Martin has ministered to and touched many lives through her spiritual journey. Academically accomplished, she holds three degrees—a Bachelor of Arts in Psychology/Education and Sociology, and a Master of Arts in Counseling. She plans to pursue a doctoral degree in Biblical Studies, as God permits. She is also an entrepreneur, having founded her own business, Catherine Creations, in October 2024—a venture she considers a true blessing from God. Her business is located at 113 N. College Street, Wallace, North Carolina.

The Unrevealing Shadow Walker: Uncover Your Eyes to See the Reality of the Mask of Lies is her debut book, written under divine guidance to share her story and meet the needs of those seeking truth and healing.

Prophetess Catherine L. Martin was born and raised in Newark, New Jersey, by her late parents, James C. Hardy Sr. and Mary L. Hardy. She now resides in North Carolina with her loving husband, Mr. Kevin J. Martin. Together, they have three adult children—Ja'Quan S. Scott, Steven T. Sweeney Jr., and Daziyah P. Rosebure—and are blessed with seven beautiful grandchildren: Zo'lin Scott, Mazi Scott, Saahirah Tamia Sweeney, Royal Sweeney, Nevaeh Sweeney, Queen, and the late Sincere T. Sweeney Jr. (deceased October 26, 2020), along with five bonus grandchildren.

www.ingramcontent.com/pod-product-compliance
Lightning Source LLC
Chambersburg PA
CBHW050729010526
44107CB00009B/788